ARTIA

OLGA ŠROŇKOVÁ

GOTHIC

WOMAN'S

FASHION

OLGA ŠROŇKOVÁ

GOTHIC WOMAN'S FASHION

ARTIA

PRAGUE

CONTENTS

LIST OF ILLUSTRATIONS

9

INTRODUCTION

The aim of this book is to draw attention to a specially interesting chapter in the history of feudal fashion, which is illustrated by a series of works of art, of sculptures, paintings, and illuminated manuscripts, which show in detail the changes in fashion as they occurred in Bohemia during the Middle Ages, and which give us not only contemporary illustrations of fashion but also suggest just why these fashions arose when they did.

These remarkable changes in Bohemian fashion took place at a time when Bohemia was famous for the riches of her silver mines, at a time when, thanks to astute trade agreements, international trade flourished, when mutual relations between East and West, North and South were cleverly encouraged by the policy of the Luxembourg dynasty, founded by the last of the knight-errants, King Jan of Luxembourg, and were finally brought to perfection by the statesmanship of his diplomat son, the emperor Charles IV. International trade was carried on, though on a smaller scale, by his grandson, the extravagant Wenceslas IV. The close of the Luxembourg period coincided with the Hussite period marking the first great social revolutionary movement in Europe.

The hundred years of fashion thus under consideration fall into four periods in which fashion was dominated by the movements initiated by the three monarchs mentioned above and by the people's Hussite movement. In connection with this development Bohemian fashion achieved a remarkable perfection and became the leading fashion in Central Europe.

The expression "fashion" as understood now-a-days did not originate until as late as the 15th century, but this by no means suggests that prior to that time clothing did not undergo any changes, and that thus fashion did not exist, for "fashion is the daughter of the many-sided spirit of every civilised nation and shares the fate of all human changes", as a Venetian senator of the 14th century said; fashion has always existed and will always continue to exist.

The reader can easily find in the dictionary that the word *mode* for fashion is derived from the Latin *modus*. Further the dictionary will tell the reader that the word acquired its modern meaning, *viz.* changes in wearing apparel, in France in the 15th century. However, dictionaries do not provide any explanation why this change in the meaning of the word arose just in the 15th century, and yet it is a most interesting question in itself.

Keys of modern dictionaries when mentioning fashion agree that fashion is an accompanying phenomenon of all stages of development of culture. Accordingly the antique period had a fashion of its own as had also the feudal period.

The illustrations selected from the rich store of miniatures found in Bohemian illuminated manuscripts and in Bohemian tempera paintings on wood show details from these so as to give the reader an idea of all sides of women's fashion, its accessories as well as the materials of which the garments were made. It is not usual to give these details separately in books on fashion, and still less in books on costume. We have chosen to show these details also in the hope of arousing the reader's interest in a little known chapter in the history of women's garments.

We examine both the sleeve of the garment and the design of the collar, the figure, the placing of the girdle, the style of the skirt, the trimmings on the bodice and even the bed-linen and personal lingerie. The pictorial material should thus enable the reader to gain a clear and detailed idea of the fashion of the whole of the Gothic period, which may be said to be the really creative and determining period for fashion as we know it today. It was the period which adapted to needs, and which produced not only remarkable garments for the higher strata of society but also a simple garment and a working garment which proved its usefulness for many centuries. The fundamental principles (i. e. what modern fashion calls line) make themselves most felt in the simplest and not in the most elaborate garments.

It may come as a surprise to readers acquainted with books on fashion that we dwell so much on the simplest of garments, but as we hope to show it is these garments which are of special importance for our problem. They have something "eternal" about them as far as both style and pattern of material are concerned. In the present age of standardisation this fact is of double interest.

THE MEDIEVAL PERIOD

In order better to understand the development of Bohemian fashion in the later Middle Ages it will be best first to devote a short chapter to the early medieval period. The characteristic feature of early medieval fashion is its peculiar conservatism. It remained still faithful to the fashion of Christian antiquity with the result that elements in it survived for so long as to be taken over almost unchanged by Gothic fashion; the principal parts of the dress with which this was the case were the veil and cloak.

On the whole it may be said that the fashion of Bohemia between the year 1090 and the first quarter of the 13th century resembled in principle the antique fashion but was influenced by Byzantine fashion. The Byzantine influence was, however, more apparent in the trimmings and material than in the style and the character of the dress.

This is already brought out by the garment of the Princess Emma from the so-called Gumpold Legend about St. Wenceslas. The manuscript which we have of this Legend was written about 1006 for Princess Emma herself; she was the wife of Boleslav II, and it was her father who ordered the assassination of St. Wenceslas.

The title page shows St. Wenceslas and at his feet, in deep humility, lies Princess Emma herself. Her garment consists of an undergarment with tight-fitting sleeves. The borders should be noticed here. In principle this is a well-known type of garment. It is traditionally said to have been introduced by the Byzantine Princess Theofana. Over the undergarment Princess Emma wears a long cloak with gilt bordering at the neck and at the bottom hem. The head is covered with a closely fitting veil formed into a corner at the back.

The deep emotion evinced by Princess Emma and her prayer for forgiveness at the feet of the Saint is expressed by Byzantine gesture, by the prostration of the figure. The cloak and its folds falling over the rim of our picture reveal the roundness of knees and the straight line of the back. The cloak veils the figure from neck to heel. It becomes a part of the figure, it envelops it, it forces itself on us as a substitute for the figure of which we are no longer aware. The cloak resembles a disguise behind which the woman almost vanishes. From the historical point of view it is, of course, an antique drapery, a surviving remnant of the former antique period. The hierarchic Byzantine period contributed details consisting of rules of adornment and etiquette. These rules emphasised the purpose of the garment with due regard to its social function. The type of garment worn by Princess Ema is typical for imperial garments. The gilt border of the cloak and veil was an indispensable and prescribed part of the Byzantine cloak. During the 8th to 10th centuries it spread to the rest of Europe as a mark of royal rank.

The Byzantine fashion with its minutely prescribed details probably appealed to the taste of the time, and the differences in detail of garment indicate the status of its wearer in the hierarchy of early feudal society in Europe.

Material played a specially important rôle in this period. Although the early medieval stylised representation does not permit us to recognise with certainty the material of which Princess Emma's cloak was made, we may surmise that it was of silk. Its apparently dotted pattern is reminiscent of the patterns of Byzantine materials interwoven with gold threads of the 8th to 10th centuries.

Because the style of this type of dress — by this we mean its rather uninteresting cut — remained actually unchanged throughout the early Middle Ages, the quality of the material used became the distinctive character of the garment of the various classes. The Byzantine silk was in the early medieval period the mark of the higher social strata. These materials, as we know, reached Western and Central Europe mainly in the form of gifts. Later these precious materials were either brought back as spoils of war, as for instance during the Crusades, or found their place in the international trade between East and West.

I.

IMPERIAL DRESS FROM ABOUT THE YEAR 1000
Detail of title page.

Legend of St. Wenceslas (written by Gumpold, Bishop of Mantua at the wish of Emperor Otto II).
Illuminated copy made at the order of Princess Emma, wife of Boleslav II, between 1000 and 1006.
Manuscript of the School of Fulda.

Former Ducal Library at Wolfenbüttel.

17

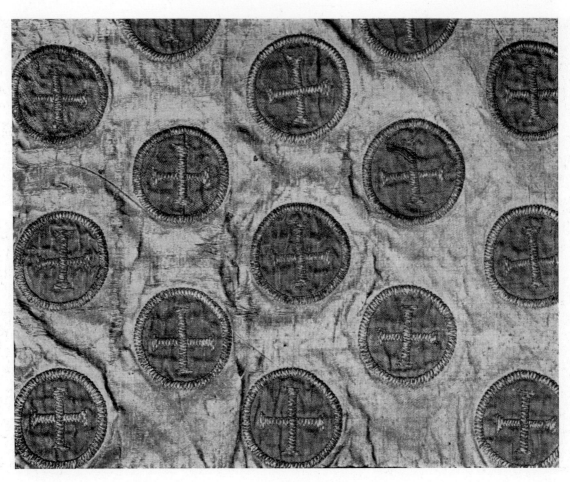

2.

SILK MATERIAL WITH APPLICATION FROM THE COVER OF THE TOMB
OF ST. WENCESLAS,

first half of the 12th century.
First mentioned in the inventory of 1387 of the Prague Cathedral of St. Vitus.

Prague, Municipal Museum.

Precious remnants of these materials, preserved mainly as church treasures, are usually adorned with geometric or circular ornaments with stylised animal-motifs and plant motifs, or with for instance starlets as secondary motifs.

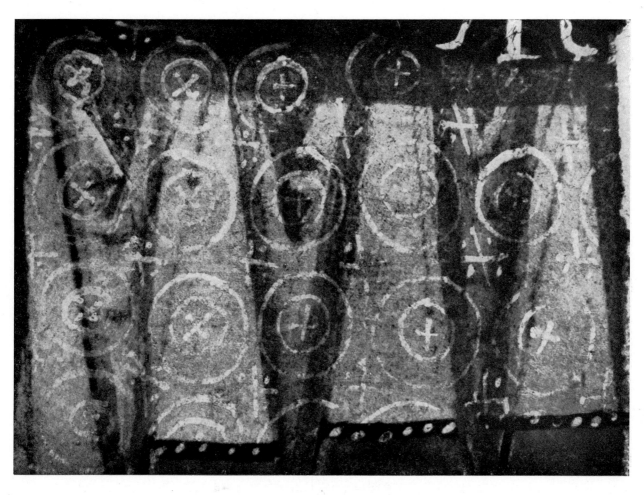

3.

SAMPLE OF MATERIAL
Detail of the initial I (the prophet Haggai and Frater Godefridus), f. 171, The Bible of St. Francis,
from the end of the 13th century.

The manuscript belonged to the Franciscan monastery in Old Town,
founded in 1234 together with the Clarissan convent; it is the earliest Gothic building in Prague.
Prague, Library of the National Museum, sign. XII B·13.

St. Vitus Cathedral in Prague possesses still a splendid remnant of an oriental cover with applications and embroideries from the middle of the 12th century. The characteristic feature of this is the division into circles which are filled by a motif of crosslets. According to tradition it covered the coffin of St. Wenceslas. Thus it became a relic in itself, and it acquired such fame as to be frequently copied.

4.

SAMPLE OF MATERIAL

Detail of a miniature on f. 346 of the manuscript of the "On the Death of a High-Spirited Youth", from the first quarter of the 15th century.

Almanac of Religious Treatises known as the Krumlov Almanac.
Prague, Library of the National Museum, III B 10.

We find thus the above design almost exactly copied in the St. Francis' Bible from the end of the 13th century, and even as late as the 15th century we find painters of miniatures and paintings on wood again returning to this relic.

It is relatively rare in the early medieval period to find a painter decorating his work of art with representations of historical persons of his own time; and when he does so, he represents only his patrons, emperors and empresses, ladies-in-waiting etc. It was only very rarely that the artist chose to paint a person of a less exalted station in life. In various Bohemian pictures of the early Middle Ages we can, however, detect some social differences, although these are not shown by either the plural character of the dress or by its style but only by its elaborateness. It is also more clearly shown in illuminated manuscripts and in wall-paintings, where recent changes appear sooner than in plastic material, whether bronze or stone, and where the dependence on the style of antiquity was greater. Even here, however, we find social distinctions clearly expressed. Recent changes in fashion are thus very well shown in the reliefs of the well known bronze door of the cathedral at Gnesen in Poland (about 1150).

Previously scholars dealing with the history of fashion had vainly searched for objects of art which would yield proofs of the social differences in clothing mentioned in the literary sources (Vincencius), but the reliefs of the doors of Gnesen give incontrovertible proofs of their existence.

The reliefs show the legend of the second Bohemian saint, St. Adalbert. His mother belonged to the nobility, and the relief of her shows a carefully finished-off garment with rich borders. Under the outer garment we catch a glimpse of an undergarment; moreover she is presented as wearing the type of sandals introduced by the revival of Byzantine fashion and has a veil covering her hair.

St. Adalbert's mother is accompanied by servants, bareheaded and barefooted maids. Their upper garments are a little shorter than that of their mistress and without any borders. In principle their garment is of the same chemise-like style as that of their mistress. This chemise-like style is usually considered to be the second stage in the development of cut in general; it is still used in the men's dress of the national costumes in this country, for example in Slovakia. It is made of one strip of material with a hole cut for the head. The single width of material of which the garment is made is practically of the same size irrespective of the size of the person for whom the garment is made. Thus it is not quite accurate to speak of any cut here, as the material is simply sewn together.

The sculptor of the Gnesen reliefs belonged to the Bohemian circle of 11th century artists best known from a number of beautifully illuminated manuscripts, the most famous of which is the *Codex vyšehradský*. The illuminations in this manuscript are outstanding for their richness, clarity and expressiveness (Květ). The illuminations show an astounding variety of styles of dress, and may even be said to furnish examples of every conceivable style used at the time. As the illuminations moreover present a great number of different persons, all of them dressed differently, the dresses shown in the illuminations have become the subject of special treatment. Our reproductions show the garment of a working woman and of one belonging to the nobility. The garment of the serf or working woman is exceptionally well shown in the dress of the maid servants in St. Peter's Denial of the Lord. Like the dress of the maids in the St. Adalbert Legend it consists of a straight outer garment reaching to the ankles with wide sleeves and a veil or rather a shawl of a simple rectangular shape.

The garment of the mistress is in the same plain style. The material is, however, sewn together with bordered hems. The borders are speckled with small golden plates and semi-precious stones. It might be possible to consider this abundance of ornamentation as the last traces of the gradually waning desire for splendour and luxury which seized the people of Europe after the end of the period of the Migration of the Nations. It is besides also the generally accepted opinion that it is possible to connect these two phenomena, remote from each other though they are in time, because fashion, as already said, changed very slowly at this time. "The appearance of women of that period is very colourful and radiant . . . Its character, however, is semi-barbarous, unelegant and unfinished . . . From various pagan, classical, antique and Byzantine elements which have not yet settled their mutual relations culture slowly began to emerge. The garment is not yet close-fitting and has no folds." (Falke)

The colourful appearance of early medieval women impresses us in a different way. We observe its structure, and see that the woman's figure creates one might almost say a block, the surface of which is divided, vertically and horizontally, into single units by bordered hems. For example the sleeves are divided from the garment by a sewn-on border, and the garment itself is divided by borders into two or four parts. We see in this division the basis of early medieval fashion. This conception corresponds to the architecture of the time, which has the same block-like character with the surface divided in a similar way by dwarfs, arcades, arched friezes, etc. It might even be said that the system of surface ornamentation in architecture is purely tectonic. Similarly, the borders on garments have a definite function. They are not a mere adornment of the garment or distinctions, as prescribed by Byzantine fashion. They either connect the material in seams or they hem it, thus helping to make it firmer. From the artistic point of view the whole of the garment remains undisturbed, it creates a more elaborate unit consisting of a large number of individual links (Birnbaum). Literature of the last century, which gave a general characterisation of the period under review, saw in this garment all the elements of the past cultures exhibited side by side. We should rather say that early medieval fashion like early medieval visual art created at this stage its own style corresponding to its own ideal.

The transition period between the early and late Middle Ages of women's garments corresponds roughly to the period of transition from natural to monetary economy. In Bohemia the transition period covers roughly the years 1200—1275, while abroad it ends already about the middle of the 13th century.

The women's garment in this period still retained the tradition of the 12th century, and did not free itself either from the early medieval style or from its rich adornment. It still consisted of a draped undergarment reaching to the ankles and of a shorter dress, as we have already seen this illustrated in the bronze door of Gnesen.

5.

LEGEND OF ST. ADALBERT
Bronze relief on the door of the Cathedral of Gnesen in Poland.
About 1150.

Important monument of the Romanesque metal work in Central Europe,
indicating ancient connections between Poland and Prague.
Detail from Birth of St. Adalbert.

6. WORKING DRESS OF THE EARLY MEDIEVAL PERIOD
Detail of the illumination on f. 41a, St. Peter's Denial of the Lord.
Coronation Gospel Book, known as the Vyšehrad Codex.

The manuscript was written for the coronation of the Bohemian King Vratislav in 1085.
The manuscript, which is exceptionally richly illuminated, is the work of a Bohemian scribal workshop which produced several other sumptiously illuminated manuscripts.

Formerly the property of the Cathedral of St. Vitus and the Cathedral of Vyšehrad in Prague.
Prague, National and University Library, XIV A 13.

7.

ELABORATE DRESS FROM THE EARLY MEDIEVAL PERIOD

Detail of the illumination on f. 19b, The Sacrifice in the Temple from the coronation Gospel Book.

During the transition period, however, an important new feature made its appearance in the form of a wrap (cloak pulled over the head). This cloak is already well known from the antique period, for instance from Etruscan paintings. Now it was taken up again for later to become the universal garment of women. It reached down to the ground. Some authors believe that even fashion attempted to approach the antique ideal. Indeed, fashion like the Gothic portal sculptures from the end of the 14th century, aimed since that time at achieving a truly classic balance, which compels us to compare it with antiquity.

It was during this time that the different types of the current secular, religious and royal gowns were developed. As our example we choose the most typical of the three types, the garment of nuns, which is almost identical with the contemporary secular and royal garments, and which has remained almost unchanged since then. It consists of an undergarment with narrow sleeves, over the shoulders is a cloak, the head is covered by a veil, falling down on to the shoulders. The wimple is tucked under the veil and lies close to the neck.

The strict formality of the dress may be explained by its origin being due to the church regulation that a cloak covering the shoulders had to be worn in church. It was only during this century that the prescribed garment became the garment of married women as well as of nuns, the former, however, were not as yet obliged to keep their head covered.

Due to the advance made in the division of labour, and also due to social differentiation, clothing became more elaborate. Beginning with the early Gothic period dresses were no longer made at home, but by experts — by professional tailors.

Some historical sources describe this production in the early medieval period in Bohemia as being prior to the establishment of the guilds (*Regesta,* vol. I, 124). According to this theory there were in Prague as well as in other big towns of Bohemia big workshops where women wove, span and sewed garments. Such a shop was known as a *gyneceum*. It is said that in the 10th century there were thus employed about 30 dressmakers in the Prague castle. It is further believed that tailors worked in shops which produced garments for men. Naturally they were not artisans in the present sense of the word but serfs who made the garments of the household on the premises.

It is believed that during visits to country castles some of the surplus garments thus made were distributed among the population. According to other reports it may be supposed that later there were workshops in the country castles in Bohemia, and that the completed garments were sent to Prague. According to records from the 13th century there was a wholesale marketing of finished garments in Prague. For instance trousers were packed in parcels of forty.

A brotherhood of tailors or a tailors' guild was recognised in 1318, but already in 1283 we find the tailors as an organised group welcoming King Wenceslas I at his coronation. The tailors' guilds supplied not only the markets but made mainly men's garments to have them on stock when needed, for example by the Old Town municipality. Supplies of garments were kept in stock in case of war (Wagenknecht).

8.

DRESS OF A NUN

Detail from the initial "P". Sedlec antiphonary. First half of the 13th century.
The manuscript was made for a convent in Bohemia.

Prague, National and University Library, XIII A 6.

Tailors' guilds came to play a great rôle in the production of garments as soon as it became customary to use expensive materials and still more so when the chemise-like style was abandoned. According to one group of authors this change occurred in France in the 13th century, according to another group of authors in Italy (Deruisseau) in the 14th century. In Bohemia a period of social differentiation began in the 13th century. This tendency towards differentiation also made itself felt in clothing, where we now get garments prescribed for married women, and for unmarried women, and festival and everyday garments. It is typical for the Gothic period that one fashion succeeded the other relatively quickly; the new element which began to penetrate into fashion may be summed up as the underlining of the human figure by the dress worn, which was now made to measure for the first time.

These changes can be followed in the *Passion Book of Abbess Kunhuta* (about 1320), which constitutes the first of the many beautiful Bohemian manuscripts of the Gothic period. For our purpose this Passion Book is very important as it may be regarded as a repertory of women's fashions. It contains all types of contemporary women's garments and gives a good survey of the Bohemian fashion of the first quarter of the 14th century.

Thus already the title page shows us the gown of the nuns of the Benedictine order from the oldest convent in Bohemia, the St. George's Convent on the Hradčany. The gown is conservative in style and practically the same as in the preceding period. It consisted, as it still consists, of an undergarment with tight-fitting sleeves, over which is worn an ungirded gown with wide sleeves and over this again a loose-hanging cloak. Two garments with a cloak, as were customary in the early medieval period, is in the Gothic period a sheer anachronism.

Gothic fashion exerted a great influence on all the component parts of the secular garment, it reduced the number of garments worn by combining the second garment with the undergarment, but it was powerless to effect any change in the traditional and strict ecclesiastic rule of a thorough veiling of the woman's figure when it came to the garment of nuns. Their garment is further a reminder of the Byzantine-early medieval conception of garment according to which the greater the number of garments worn the higher the social position of the woman. It was in fact in the early Gothic period that the power of the secular rulers became transferred to the Church. The Gothic Church provided Christ's brides with three garments and added a ceremonial cloak as suitable for the highest social strata. The medieval world conception based on hierarchy and strict differentiation of society began to influence fashion. All figures in this illustration have the same pose, thus probably expressing the strictness of the church ceremonial, valid, without exception, for all the nuns.

On the other hand, how many various poses, gestures and ways of holding the garment do we find in the following illustration showing in the scene *Ecclesia militans* virgins as well as married women. With what elegance of pose and garment the painter paints unmarried young women. The Gothic fashion ideal reaches here almost its climax. This pose was originally explained by fashion literature as being due to the tightness of the dress. Later writers have suggested that it was an outcome of a certain fashionable eccentricity. Present opinion may be summarised approximately as follows: the Gothic pose, i. e. the S-shaped bending, expresses best the Gothic ideal of the human body and brings out Gothic fashion.

9.

NUNS' DRESS

Passion Book of Abbess Kunhuta. Manuscript ordered by Abbess Kunhuta about 1320, abbess of the Convent of St. George on the Hradčany in Prague, daughter of the Bohemian king Přemysl Otakar II. The title page shows Abbess Kunhuta with the writer of the Passion Book, Kolda, and Beneš, its illuminator, and several nuns.

Detail from f. 1b.
Prague, National and University Library, sign. XIV A 17.

10.

DRESS OF UNMARRIED WOMEN, ABOUT 1320
Detail of an illumination from Ecclesia militans on f. 22b.
Passion Book of Abbess Kunhuta. Cp. no. 9.

The garment of unmarried girls in our illustration has been completely "modernised", i. e. it is entirely Gothic. Free from the early medieval adornment it owes its impressiveness mainly to its tightness, i. e. cut. The slightly tucked undergarment with a belt, heart-shaped or round neckline and narrow sleeves, does not, however, as yet play the important part it was to do later. The painter's attention is more concentrated on the cloak, the cut of which is simple; it was probably made of two strips of material sewn together, and reaching to the ground (cf. Sichart);

II.

DRESS OF MARRIED WOMEN, ABOUT 1320
Detail of an illumination from Ecclesia militans on f. 22b.
Passion Book of Abbess Kunhuta. Cp. no. 9.

the draping, however, now shows many variations. The many possibilities of variation constitute one of the greatest charms of this fashion. The right hand probably held the cloak raised, the left hand held the undergarment when walking. Even when standing motionless the corner of the cloak is lifted fairly high and thrown over the hand. The lifted corner is the most essential adornment of the Gothic outer garment of women, and the way in which it is held raised shows the elegance of the woman.

31

From the present point of view it is a very important factor. It was the first fashion to give the wearer an opportunity to exercise individual taste, and the taste of the individual plays such an important part in fashion, especially in the more advanced stages of its various cycles of development. In fact, individual taste abolishes the uniformity of appearance, while at the same time it creates fashion and brings new ideas to it.

There are many explanations as to why the lifted corner of the cloak became an integral part of Gothic fashion. Many experts are of the opinion that the women's cloaks of that time were too long, and thus had to be lifted. This explanation is purely functional. Others believe that in the preceding centuries outer garments were shorter than undergarments, and that both garments were visible. After the lengthening of the cloak both garments became equally long. By lifting the corner of the cloak it was possible to show the precious materials of both the under and outer garments and the harmony of their colours (Falke).

To this comes also the artistic aspect, which asserts itself consistently in Gothic fashion.

The buckle, a sign of dignity, is an important detail. The buckle goes back to very ancient times naturally. We have seen it in the men's garments from the early medieval period, where the buckle was worn either on the left or right side. Similarly, the Greek chiton was hooked up with an ornamental agraffe. In the Gothic fashion the buckle of the woman's garment has, however, a symbolic meaning. It is a sign of honourable women. In the 11th century at Marseilles for instance prostitutes were forbidden to have their cloaks hooked with a buckle (Steinman).

Further there are differences in the head-dress. There are rules as to the head-dress of unmarried girls and married women. These rules were observed even in a much later period, at any rate in certain social strata. Loose-hanging, long and wavy hair adorned with small crowns, wreaths and metal rings are typical for unmarried girls. Hair covered with a veil is a sign of married women. In 1279 an ecclesiastical decree forbade women above 18 years of age to have their heads uncovered. This decree was, however, never observed very strictly. In 1355 a new decree ordered that all women without exception had to wear veils.

Gothic fashion took over the earlier veil — an oblong strip of material, a kind of shawl — and added small edged borders to it. It loosened the tight wrapping up of the head so that the veil was now worn further back on the head. Gothic fashion acted here in a way similar to that of Gothic architecture. It took over elements of the preceding period, perfected them, and gave more freedom, softening the contour, as may be seen for example on the Gothic portal, ornamented gable and plastic crockets.

Nuns with triple rich garment, respectable women with a noble buckle, unmarried girls with wreaths, married women in veils, hooked and loose-hanging cloaks, held raised and folded into a corner, all this indicates that Gothic fashion, contrary to the preceding periods, provided a great choice of garments and trimmings, and that this choice was determined by social position or individual dignity.

12.

MODERN CLOAK WITH DECORATIVE BAND AT NECK, ABOUT 1320
Detail of an illumination on f. 3b of the parable of the gallant knight. Passion Book of Abbess Kunhuta, Cp. no. 9.

13.

WORKING DRESS OF A YOUNG WOMAN
Detail of the illustration on f. 126a from the Velislav Bible.

The manuscript was written before the middle of the 14th century for Velislav (probably the chancellor of Emperor Charles IV). Velislav is shown at the end of the manuscript kneeling before St. Catherine. Appended to the manuscript are a cycle on the Antichrist, fragments of the Passion cycle and of the Acts of the Apostles, the cycle of the Apocalypse, and the legend of St. Wenceslas. The Bible contains 747 illuminations drawn by pen.

Prague. National and University Library, sign. Lob. 412.

14.

WORKING DRESS. WITH A CLOAK

Detail of an illustration from the Velislav Bible.

35

15.

ELABORATE DRESSES OF YOUNGER WOMEN
Detail of an illustration from the Velislav Bible.
Cp. no. 13.

16.

A FASHIONABLE PLEATED CLOAK;
POSE AND ACCESSORIES SUITABLE FOR AN OLDER LADY,
FROM THE MIDDLE OF THE 14th CENTURY
Detail of an illustration from the Velislav Bible.
Cp. no. 13.

36

37

Further details in the Gothic fashion then developed within the given frame of social differentation. At first sight the garment of a princess does not show any great differences from that of any other unmarried girl. However, it has a number of details not to be seen in the garment of others. The basic difference is probably the small golden crown on the head. This is later subject to many prohibitions and rules of class divisions laid down by the Church. In addition to these strict regulations moralists in Bohemia as elsewhere demanded emphatically that people of different social classes be differentiated by means of dress. For example, these moralists forbade townspeople to wear rich golden trimmings, crowns and belts, reserving these for the highest strata only. There are many differences in other details too; for example the cloak is trimmed with fur so that it creates a kind of shawl collar when buttoned up. Instead of a buckle, the cloak may be fastened by a cord which is, according to present opinion, more practical than a buckle. The cloak may be worn either open, thrown back, thus permitting more freedom of movement, or pulled tightly round the figure.

Although the Passion Book of Abbess Kunhuta proved to be very instructive for our purpose, it did not show the line in Gothic fashion. This is shown, however, in the Velislav Bible from approximately the middle of the 14th century. This manuscript shows clear traces of the French school of illumination, and the fashion depicted in its illuminations is also strongly influenced by France. Here we find in their complete form all the indications which we have traced of the development of fashion in the first half of the century. It almost looks as if the illuminators had paid special attention to women's garments with the result that the illuminations give us an almost exhaustive catalogue of Gothic fashion. The manuscript brings us also a whole series of garments showing the difference of clothing for the different classes of society. It introduces us to new types of women's garments (*surcoats*), and the most complicated adjustments of veils and head-bands, more current in France than in the more staid countries of Central Europe. The basis of this new fashion is best seen in the plainest garment — the working garment. The women's working garment from the middle of the 14th century, as shown in the Velislav Bible, is a flowing, ungirded gown, tight-fitting above the waist. It has a rather small oval neckline and tight-fitting long sleeves. This simple garment forms the basis for the whole of Gothic fashion as far as women are concerned. Its line is undisturbed by any girdle, it is straight, uninterrupted like the pillars of contemporary architecture. It is a basic Gothic tendency which here asserts itself, as it did in all the arts and crafts of the period. Thus we may consider the working garment as showing the simplest Gothic cut. It was the all day and every day garment of the lower strata of society and the night garment of the higher strata. For the first time since antiquity the outline of the body was stressed, for the garment is made to fit tightly to the body, although at the same time it also allows freedom of movement. In fact, both early medieval garments and Gothic garments are outstanding as the simplest of garments.

17. DRESSES WITH THE MOST UP-TO-DATE ACCESSORIES FROM THE
MIDDLE OF THE 14th CENTURY
Detail of an illustration from the Velislav Bible. Cp. no. 13.

A cloak is sometimes thrown over this garment. Working women pulled this up over their head, thus improvising a kind of hood. Women of the higher social strata wore it raised so that it fell into the inevitable corner. In the Velislav Bible this cloak stands stiffly up at the back of the neck suggesting a collar, but this is a mere French eccentricity, and it took a long time before it became generally adopted.

The open cloak reveals either a plain or a more elaborate gown. The latter is also ungirded, but fits tighter to the body than the former. The feminine figure is underlined by horizontal folds modelling the bust. Below the waist these folds become a richness of vertical folds, probably formed by sewn-in wedges, while the tight fit round the waist and hips is retained.

Although the working garment remained the basis of all Gothic fashion, the elaborate garment exploited all the suggestions inherent in its early development. The figure is shown still more clearly, because the dress has come to fit more tightly, the vertical lines in the cut of the skirt are brought out all the more clearly by the contrasting horizontal lines of the folds of the bodice. It is even said that the dress was so tight that it barely allowed breathing.

The most important accessories of the elaborate garment were ornaments and head covers. The unmarried girl had long flowing hair with a garland. The married woman of the nobility wore for instance a high head-band, later to become the Renaissance beret, connected with a net which covered the entire head-dress. Wimple (French *guimple*, German *Gebende*) running under the chin and holding the beret firmly in place (cp. Matějček, Velislav Bible), as worn by some of the women in the Velislav Bible, was probably a French invention; it was not generally used in Central Europe until much later. It is obvious from one of the illuminations in the Velislav Bible that in Bohemia a Gothic lady preferring a more sober style of dress might wear only a simple veil falling down on to the shoulders.

The tight-fitting gown of a young woman from the Velislav Bible shows us how Gothic style completed the development of fashion that had taken place in the previous age, perfecting all parts of the dress, its line, its general design no less than the ornaments that went with it, and how especially it transformed the veil. The deep neckline underlining the bust finds its counterpart in the elaborate head-dress. The high zig-zag head-dress is developed till it becomes grossly out of proportion to the rest. This fashion spread to such an extent in Italy that municipal authorities issued one prohibition after another against it (Floerke).

The head-dress is for Gothic fashion what the capital of the pillar is for Gothic architecture, a motif to be played with, to elaborate, to be cherished as summing up all the other motifs. The basic line of the garment makes itself felt in each detail. The cuff of the sleeve ends in a point, the part of the sleeve above the elbow forms a liripipe which hangs free of the elbow and reaches to the ground; the shoes, too, end in a point. Thus each part of the dress forms a unit of its own, and in its own way emphasises the vertical line. The persons conform to the style and underline it by the pose of the fingers of the hand held so as to make each finger show its tapering form.

18. DRESS WITH SURCOAT. ECCENTRIC MODERN DRESS FOR
BOHEMIA IN THE FIRST HALF OF THE 14th CENTURY
Detail of the illustration on f. 12a of the Velislav Bible. Cp. no. 13.

41

Moreover Gothic fashion developed in every way and in every detail the principles suggested by the working garment. It emphasised its femininity both by its tight fit and deep neckline as well as by its various details. It invented cuffs, corners on the cloaks and sleeves, it made the shoes turn up in a point. One of its great discoveries is the cunning utilisation of the veil, specially used, of course, by those who were getting on in years. The elaborately arranged veil with its embroidered net may be regarded as a forerunner of the incoming French eccentricities. These begin to make their appearance at the beginning of the 15th century, and are well illustrated by the *Très riches heures* of the Duke of Berry as well as by English brasses.

The climax of fashion presented by the illuminators of the Velislav Bible is shown in the dress of Sarah. Here we meet for the first time a new piece of clothing, which came to play a great part in the further development of fashion. It is a tight-fitting short coat with narrow sleeves, and it is made of another colour than the undergarment; it is the so-called *surcoat (surcotium)*. In Bohemia this short coat had sleeves, while the French, the English and Italian surcoats had none. The low-cut neckline of the surcoat as well as of the gown underlines the femininity of the figure. However, to meet all moral requirements the neck is covered by a fine veil cut in a curve so as to leave only a small part of the throat free.

From the point of view of fashion the Velislav Bible presents the end of a process the beginning of which is represented by the Passion Book of Abbess Kunhuta. Fashion had brought out the basic lines of the figure by creating a tight-fitting garment, and thus it shows us how the realistic tendency of the Gothic age made itself felt also in fashion.

The knightly fashion of the John of Luxembourg period had the purity, grace and monumentality of the continental Gothic of its age, and it is all shown to us in the drawings of the Velislav Bible. The masterly conception of this branch of miniature drawing presents Gothic fashion as if it were a completed sculptural or even architectural work of art. Folds of the derided and persecuted Gothic train form a kind of base for the harmonising vertical folds of the skirt. Out of them grows the fragile body, carrying the head adorned with rich fashionable accessories, completing the figure as the ornamented capital of a column completes the column. The moralists of the period hated the fresh richness of details with its corners, points, wimples and veils; the 19th century laughed at it; it is only now that we fully appreciate its logic, its extremely vivid contact with reality, and recognise it for what it is: the most elegant fashion of all centuries. Its relation to art is perfectly balanced by its relation to nature. The suppleness of the woman's body is discovered with the same delight as the age discovered flowers, birds and fruits.

Gothic fashion is the most accomplished fashion of all time. The problem of style and detail is solved with the same logic as in any other work of art of the time. All the component elements taken over from the preceding period, e. g. the cloak, are transformed by its genius to conform to the taste of the new age (see the cloak) and made in a new medium (see the veil) thus fulfilling new functions.

I. CURRENT GOTHIC CLOAKS, THEIR CLASPS AND CORDS

Madonna with St. Catherine and St. Margaret; about 1360.

Tempera painting on spruce, h. 95 cm., w. 101.5 cm. České Budějovice. Municipal Museum.

John of Luxembourg had brought Bohemia to the forefront in international relations; the army of Bohemia was feared on the battle field and the statesmanship of her ruler was acclaimed in the council chambers all over Europe. Fashion in Bohemia in this period reflected truly the rôle played by the country. It shows new forms, gathered from many European countries, as indeed we have already seen it illustrated in the Passion Book of Abbess Kunhuta and in the Velislav Bible. With the reign of Charles IV, the illustrious son of his famous father, a period of stabilisation set in; and fashion reflected this too. After the venturesomeness of the John of Luxembourg period, after its sometimes uncritical acceptance of French fashion, the fashion of the period of Charles IV expresses the self-reliance, the awareness of its own worth, and the splendour which by right belonged to it as the fashion of a great country ruled by a wise king. A certain moderation of the fashion eccentricities set in all over Europe, and the 14th century has become known in fashion as the period of "noble classic fashion" (Falke).

John of Luxembourg had established specially close relations with France, and during his reign many new fashions in literature, in architecture as well as in dress came to Bohemia from France. Charles IV maintained the tradition of close relations with France, but in addition he developed relations too with Italy, and above all he re-established the tradition of close contact with the East. Perhaps it was partly due to the fresh impulses thus received that fashion acquired its character of splendour during his reign. It is also well known that the fashion of the court of Charles IV most of all influenced the fashion of the court of Richard II at Westminster and was brought to England in 1382 by the Bohemian Princess Anne, wife of Richard II.

The manysidedness of the genius of Charles IV is reflected not only in his building activity and the beauty of the buildings with which he adorned his beloved Prague but in the entire cultural life of his time, including fashion. His main interest was to ensure a sound ecconomic basis for the new life he so zealously fostered. He re-established Prague as the centre of international trade, he not only caused the precious products elsewhere to be imported into Bohemia but made Bohemia itself a centre of production, not only of cloth but also of many other goods. All this gave of course an impetus to the development of fashion. The King-Emperor Charles IV encouraged art as well as learning, and during his reign painting and sculpture developed greatly. The splendid buildings which he built were decorated in a manner worthy of them with cycles of paintings by the best Bohemian masters of the age.

When we look at the illustrations given here, we must not, however, forget that we use the paintings and sculptures for a special purpose, and that in reality they form an integral part of a great and harmonious whole.

·Margareta Imparrix·;· Elyzabeth Regi·mat Karoli·;· Anna Impatr Regis F

19.

Portraits of Bohemian queens in ceremonial shoulder-cape — mark of royal power.
Detail of an illustration from the Chronicon aulae regiae of 1391—1393.

Jihlava, Municipal Archives.

The magnificent paintings of the time of Charles IV enable us to examine the fashion of his period in detail, and give us not only an opportunity to admire the elegance of the figures, the design and charm of the garments, but also the precious materials out of which they were made, and the goldsmith's art lavished on the jewellery. The paintings give us further an opportunity to examine the individual parts of the dress in detail, the cloak and wimple no less than the sleeve and neckline and the jewellery so much loved by the age. In order, however, to show these details and follow their development it will be necessary to deal with each detail separately instead of confining ourselves to one series of paintings at a time, thus achieving continuity of subject and follow its development as exhibited in the various paintings and sculptures. We have no longer any manuscripts to give us a detailed presentation of fashion, but instead we have other splendid works of art, portraits of private persons as well as paintings of the Virgin and saints.

II. BROCADES AND HANGINGS FROM THE MIDDLE
OF THE 14th CENTURY

From the Annunciation of the Virgin (about 1350) of the Master of Vyšší Brod.
Tempera painting on wood, h. 95 cm., w. 85.5 cm.

The picture is part of a cycle of nine panels with scenes from the life and suffering of Christ, which were kept until World War II in the Cistercian Abbey at Vyšší Brod (Southern Bohemia), whence they were caried off to Germany during the German occupation of Czechoslovakia. Today Prague, National Gallery. Author: The Master of Vyšší Brod, called so after the home of the painting, Vyšší Brod, where since 1259 there has been a Cistercian monastery. Before the middle of the 14th century the probable donor of the cycle, Peter of Rožmberk, entered the order; he was one of the outstanding feudal lords of Bohemia in the first half of the 14th century.

They are all dressed in the same way, and the saints are even more elegant than the princesses. Thus it is possible to use indifferently paintings with religious and secular subjects for our purpose — as has indeed long been recognised.

The painting of the Virgin between St. Catharine and St. Margaret from about 1360 may serve as an example of many other paintings of the period. Here both saints show the pose and spirit of young women of the nobility. Both saints are painted as if they were princesses; they wear crowns (one crown with high trefoils, the other with a lower décor) and have flowing hair. The worldly princesses Anna, Elisabeth etc. on a 14th century drawing are dressed much in the same way. The hair of both saints and princesses is half-long, coming to below the opening of the oval neckline, which, however, is narrower and less low-cut for the saints than for the princesses. The garment of the saints and princesses has tight-fitting sleeves which partly cover the back of the hand. The saints wear a cloak fastened across the breast by a tasselled cord. The princesses wear coats with ermine cape. Both saints and princesses hold the garment lifted either with one or both hands, thus showing us the different possibilities of opening the cloak, throwing it over one hand, spreading it out and folding the corners so that they fall down in a rich cascade of precious material. They all stand in the S-shaped position dictated by the fashion of the time. The Gothic period established a certain code of social behaviour not only of table manners, but also of manner of walking, standing, holding one's hands, and sitting as well (Falke).

This S-shaped pose is rather exaggerated in tempera paintings on wood. Drawings of the period, however, exhibit various realistic deviations from the code both as regards general bearing and pose.

It is only natural that we learn so very little about new details and fashion eccentricities from the paintings of virgins and saints. Their garments remain ceremonial. On the other hand these paintings offer an opportunity for a detailed study of line as understood by the most advanced painters of their age, and from this we may infer what was regarded as beautiful by the age.

The cloaks fitting closely to the shoulders fall in large bowl-like folds down to the waist, and thence downwards in rich folds. The tight fit of the upper part of the garment as well as the pose are prescribed by the Gothic code both for women and men — the men's garments were of a very feminine cut in the Gothic period. Below the waist the women's garment falls down in rich folds helping to mould the figure into the prescribed form. It is characteristic for the Gothic ideal of style that the open cloak reveals part of the undergarment in such a way as to make it form two triangles, the upper one pointing upwards to the neck and thus widest at the waist, while the lower one points to the waist and is thus widest at the bottom hem, both thus giving the beloved corner effect under the rich cascades of the cloak. The slimness, immateriality, of the body is emphasised in every detail, the richness of the drapery providing the necessary contrast.

Already the word drapery itself, current in all European languages and derived from the French *draper,* i. e. drape into rich folds, indicates that it was originally taken from the French *drap* (cp. Gutmann), i. e. cloth. The Flanders cloth was the basic material of the Gothic woman's garment; its use heralded a new period in the development of the Gothic cloak, which we shall have occasion to mention below.

20. PATTERN OF GOTHIC COSTLY FABRICS
Detail of an angel.

Annunciation of the Virgin, about 1350.
Master of Vyšší Brod. (Cp. sup. II.)

21. GOLDEN BORDERS AND BROCADE
Detail of an angel. Annunciation of the Virgin, about 1350.
Master of Vyšší Brod. (Cp. suppl. II and no. 20.)

21.

22.

PATTERN ON A GOTHIC PRECIOUS MATERIAL

Detail from the garment of Christ.

The Ressurrection, about 1350. Master of Vyšší Brod. Cp. suppl. II.

III.

Master of Vyšší Brod. The Ressurrection, about 1350.
Tempera painting on wood, h. 95 cm., w. 85.5 cm. (Cp. sup. II.)

Gothic fashion for women preferred cloth of one colour for the cloak and garment. Brocades and patterns are reserved in the first place for ceremonial garments.

In Italy, since the end of the 13th century, the authorities of both Church and State had endeavoured to reserve luxuriant materials for their own use. This is confirmed not only by the repeated ecclesiastical prohibitions against their use by others but also by guild regulations as well (Ferrara, 1279). According to guild regulations much more was to be demanded for making a garment of a precious material than for making one of a plain material. It seems, however, that this protection of splendour was not very effective (Floerke).

As far as Bohemia is concerned the series of paintings by the Master of Vyšší Brod shows us the most gorgeous elaborateness of garments. Almost every painting in the series exhibits a different kind of material, thus witnessing to the painter's love of splendour as well as to his almost Italian sense for rich material. This may be regarded as the first and general answer to the question of the importance of the Master of Vyšší Brod for the history of Bohemian fashion.

Like other painters of the Middle Ages he conformed to the iconographic rules according to which the Virgin is usually dressed in a classic garment of fine Flanders cloth. In this respect he contributed nothing new.

Angels, on the other hand, are dressed with the greatest worldly luxury, as is indeed in accord with the current way of presenting them at the time. Their garments, as may be seen from the Annunciation and Resurrection, show all the love of splendour and magnificence of the Italian fashion, and such garments were a constant source of disagreement with the authorities. The Angel in the Resurrection has, for example, a deep oval neckline adorned with borders studded with precious stones. He has a broad gilt girdle and gilt cuffs at the sleeves. These borders and cuffs had once before been the fashion in Bohemia; they were now introduced again from Italy; their semi-precious stones were arranged in various geometrical designs as well as in meanders, chessboard patterns and rosettes. He has pointed shoes and sleeves studded with buttons. In Italy all this is constantly being prohibited, restricted, or severely castigated. Thus for instance, from the middle of the 14th century, we know prohibitions issued in Florence summarising all the preceding ones issued in the other Central Italian towns. There is no doubt that the Master of Vyšší Brod was extremely well informed about the newest Italian fashion. He loved to use it in his paintings. This is one of the most striking proofs of his deep attachment to reality; but it was the reality of Italy not of Bohemia.

The garments of Christ and the apostles are Italian in design and almost naturalistic in their imitation of reality; their plastic pattern contrasts with the large unbroken surface of plain material, especially in the coats. Sometimes the cloaks, especially those of the angels, have patterns; but those patterns were invented by the artist, and they lack the naturalistic character of those of the cloaks of the angels. The pattern of the angel's cloak from the Annunciation is obviously a free variation on the theme of some Italian designs which were probably painted on the material rather than woven into it, but in the Czech pattern we have a greater variety of design than is given by fixed textile patterns; thus palmettes composed of rosettes, heraldic designs and Maltese crosses are found singly or together on the same material. (The painter of the Kladzko Madonna reproduced the pattern in the same way as the Master of Vyšší Brod.) The ornamentally used letter "S" (at the cloak's hem under the sleeve) may be regarded as an interesting detail. (Possibly it is a motif from a monogram.) This, too, is one of the motifs forbidden in Italy for private persons (Floerke). In our material it appears only in the 14th century in the antiphonary of Queen Elisabeth Rejčka (1317).

The apostles, Christ and the angels in this series are dressed in gowns and cloaks similar to those of princesses and saints, but their garments are usually made of brocades with rich design with gilt borders. The current patterns on the undergarments are usually composed of cinqfoils and lilies forming heart-shaped medallions arranged close together in vertical lines. The textile pattern is usually strictly adhered to in the paintings, the folds being suggested rather by the shade of colour to avoid disturbing the textile pattern. It is painted very carefully and with great fidelity as if it were a reproduction of jewellery. Indeed, the stamping on the gilt borders is actually made by a mechanical process. We find often here the heart-shaped pattern which is so characteristic of Italian brocades, and which is inspired by eastern designs (Falke). The import of these materials to Bohemia is confirmed by the material with a similar design preserved in one of the royal tombs in Prague.

23.

TWO FUNDAMENTAL TYPES OF GOTHIC PATTERNS
Detail from the garment of an apostle.

The Ascension, about 1350. Master of Vyšší Brod.
Tempera painting on wood, h. 95 cm., w. 85.5 cm. (Cp. sup. II.)

24.

GOTHIC PATTERN OF MATERIAL
Detail from the garment of one of the Magi.

Adoration of the Magi, about 1350.
Master of Vyšší Brod.

IV. Master of Vyšší Brod. Adoration of the Magi, about 1350. Tempera painting on wood, h. 95 cm., w. 85.5 cm.

The garment of the Gothic virgins and saints is usually reproduced as being of unpatterned cloth. Consequently its simplicity contrasts strongly with the decorative background, with the draperies adorning their thrones, with the cushions on which they sit or lie (cp. also the Kladzko Madonna). The Master of Vyšší Brod shows also a preference for reproducing the patterns on brocades, so much in favour in his day. When he painted undergarments, he tried to preserve the curved or rhomboid pattern filled with lilies, using for this purpose plastic imitation of brocade threads, a pattern which was also much in favour in the Early Gothic period. An almost exact parallel to this design may be found on an Italian material of the 13th century (Falke, II. Pic. Nos. 288, 290). Patterns of this kind naturally appealed to the painter of the age with his liking for decorative colourfulness and arabesque, as we see it in paintings from north of the Alps, and he lavished his skill on it. We shall see later that this manner of reproduction in paintings by which brocade is reproduced as something stiff which has to be painted in the same way as a jewel reaches its climax in the paintings with which Charles IV adorned his castle at Karlštejn. If the painter is not willing to repeat the simple design he looses the sense for the textile rapport. He fills the surface with various decorative elements, which are more a reminiscence of the Italian patterns of Lucca than a true reproduction. This vacillation between reality and free design is most apparent when the painter tries to indicate the folds of the cloak, or when he has to fill in the pattern in an already painted object, as for example the pattern of a cushion.

The painter's pattern of birds, starlets, circles, crosslets, lilies and branches is composed so as to fill the surface ornamentally. However, the typical repetition of pattern characteristic for reproduction of textile designs has not been achieved even once.

25.

TEXTILE PATTERN FREELY IMITATED IN PAINTING
Detail from the cushion of the Madonna.

Birth of Christ, about 1350.
Master of Vyšší Brod.

V. Master of Vyšší Brod. Birth of Christ. Tempera painting on wood, h. 95 cm., w. 85.5 cm.

Inventories of estates and the above-mentioned prohibitions tell of the great wealth of patterns, of rich materials favoured at that time and worn especially by fashionable Italian ladies; thus we may safely conclude that they were current in certain social strata. In Bohemia designs of these materials were reproduced best by the painter of the votive tablet of Jan Očko of Vlašim (after 1370), Archbishop of Prague. This painter is known for his realism; he portrays with great fidelity Charles IV, his son Wenceslas IV, and the donor of the tablet, Jan Očko of Vlašim. In the same way in which he devotes himself to reproduce their features he reproduces their garments. On the white and golden brocade of the cloak of Charles IV he paints the textile pattern of the real material. It is true that we do not possess any example of this pattern on the medieval materials which have come down to us, but the pattern gives in itself completely the impression of being a real pattern used at the time and not one invented by the painter. The pattern is painted without regard to the folds of the garment. From the shoulders down to the knees, from top to bottom, he paints the basic design in one line repeating itself at the bottom of the garment spread out behind the kneeling king.

The desire to give an exact reproduction of the pattern led the painter to make the garment appear more like armour plate with a pattern than like a real garment flowing and forming folds of its own.

26.

Textile pattern of the time imitated in painting.
Detail from the cloak of Charles IV. Votive Tablet of Jan Očko of Vlašim.

VI. Votive Tablet of Jan Očko of Vlašim, after 1370.

Tempera painting on lime wood, h. 181 cm., w. 96 cm.
Detail of the upper part of the painting.
The reproduction shows the tablet before restoration.

Prague, National Gallery.

It was not till the 15th century that the pomegranate became a frequently used pattern. It is shown in its earliest form on the chasuble of Archbishop Jan Očko of Vlašim. The materials reproduced on this tablet in the Archbishop's private chapel are modern. We must therefore conclude that the most modern Italian brocades were used at that time both by high ecclesiastical circles and by the court in Prague, as also was the case in France.

The reproduction of the silk brocade on the chasuble of St. Adalbert shows to what an extent these imported materials fascinated the painter of the votive tablet of Jan Očko of Vlašim. The pattern of the material with fire-birds, showing Chinese influence, captivated him to such an extent that he painted it on a fully spread surface without letting the cut interfere with it in any way, and then later he introduced the indispensable borders; he painted in the shadows, but took good care not to omit one half of a fire-bird, and he finished off the sprigs with birds of prey. The painting of the Madonna of Roudnice from about 1410 shows us for how long the dramatic forms of the animal motifs of the textile designs from Lucca continued to fascinate the Bohemian painters. It is, however, the last time for many centuries that we meet with this design, which may be connected with the fact that it was at this time that Lucca ceased to reproduce them (Hurníková).

27. Detail from the cloak of Jan Očko. Cp. Supplement VI.

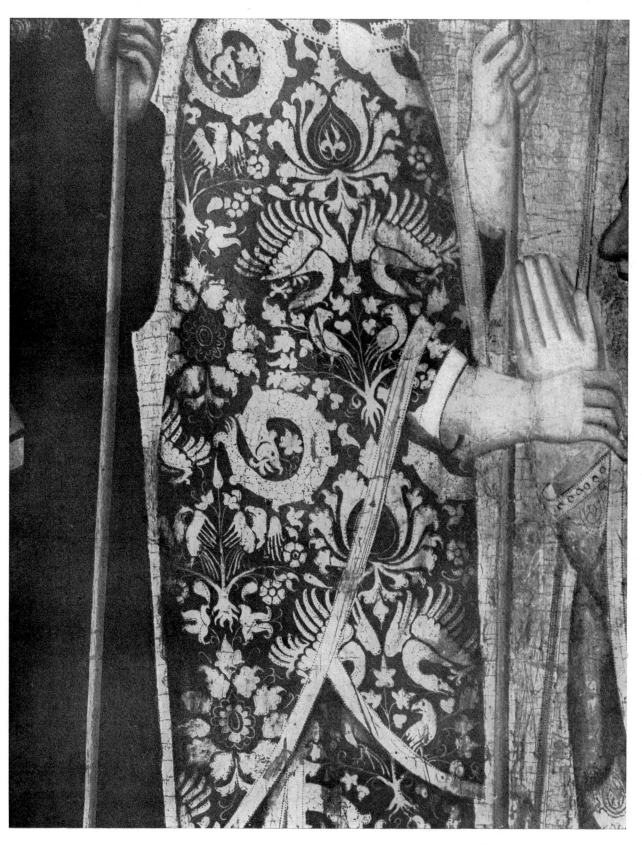

28. Detail from the cloak of St. Adalbert. Cp. Supplement VI.

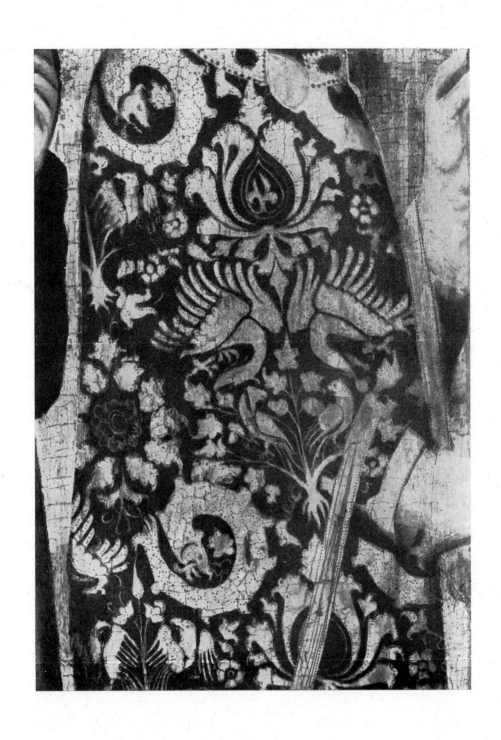

29.

Detail from the cloak of St. Adalbert. Cp. Supplement VI.

30.

Detail from the cloak of Jan Očko. Cp. Supplement VI.

CULMINATING ELEGANCE OF THE BOHEMIAN GOTHIC FASHION
FROM THE END OF THE 14th CENTURY

Most of the examples of this style which have come down to us come from the small town of Třeboň in Southern Bohemia. Třeboň gave the name to the greatest painter of the Middle Ages of Bohemia, the Master of Třeboň, and the whole school of his disciples associated with the Bohemian "Beautiful Madonnas", the most important of which is known as the Třeboň Madonna.

VII.

Master of the Třeboň Altar, about 1380.

St. Catherine, St. Magdalen, St. Margaret, Outer side of the panel, Christ on Mount Olivet.
Tempera painting on lime wood, h. 132 cm., w. 92 cm. Probably part of a former altar in St. Giles Church at Třeboň.

Prague, National Gallery.

The greatest painter of the Bohemian Middle Ages was the Master of Třeboň; he observed closely all the costly materials of his patrons' cloaks, and knew how to transfer their pattern and quality on to his paintings. However, contrary to the Master of Vyšší Brod and the painter of the votive tablet of Jan Očko of Vlašim, he paid little regard to natural decorativeness when it came to the visual function of his paintings. He is already a realist but he is not interested in arabesques. His strength lies elsewhere. He is not interested in the garment but the man whom he portrays. But even so his paintings should be mentioned in the present context, because his portraits of women show us some of the elegant creations of fashion of medieval Bohemia.

From the point of view of fashion the garments he painted are interesting by their simplicity. They envelope the woman's figure and yet reveal it as full of vitality and grace; the painting here reproduced conveys the impression of the *grande dame*. The painter has given the slim figure such tallness as almost to make it appear disproportionate. Delicate hands, arched forehead together with protruding thyroid gland incorporate the contemporary ideal without creating the impression of stylisation. The figure and the garment in which it is dressed convey the ideal of the period. Only when examining the picture more closely do we become aware of the fact that the small crown on the small head of St. Catherine emphasises the delicateness of the figure of this most elegant princess. Even without the characteristic Gothic pose it shows unmistakably the Gothic line. The gesture of the left hand holding the ribbon is typically Gothic. It gives us the impression of an almost impulsive movement captured in the moment, and not of a ceremonially determined gesture.

The type of an elderly and prudent woman is impersonated in the picture of St. Magdalen, whose head is rounder, with the hair completely covered by the veil; her cloak and its corners are thrown over the right hand.

31.

CLOAK AND GARMENT OF YOUNG WOMEN
Detail of the Madonna.

Adoration of the Child at Hluboká. Tempera painting on wood, h. 125 cm., w. 93 cm.
School of the Master of the Třeboň Altar, before 1400.

Hluboká, Castle.

31.

The figures painted by the pupils of the Master of Třeboň, in plain cloaks pulled up over the head, express by their pose, the draping of their garments and folds either joy or deep sorrow. Each detail speaks for itself, and is deliberately designed to express the content and sense of the figure. The tight sleeves, the slightly draped cloak with its wide folds suggest the tallness of the figure.

The open cloak reveals the prostrate body, the girdle placed above the waist emphasises the abdomen. At the same time the painters of the school of the Master of Třeboň are perfect experts in textile design. They know how to present cut velvet with a tiny Gothic pattern in the small rug on which the Virgin kneels. It is one of the most costly materials of its time, the use of which was not for private persons.

Cloaks pulled up over the head simplify the appearance of the figure as did the antique palla. Its uninterrupted line makes the wearer look tall and lends grandeur without any ornaments being added. Women's figures clad in this cloak appear as if hooded and absorbed in themselves.

There is actually nothing strikingly worldly or new in the garments painted by the Master of Třeboň and his pupils. We recognise all the details from the preceding period. The cloak pulled up over the head is known to us from the Passion Book of Abbess Kunhuta and from the Velislav Bible. It was taken over without alteration by the period of Charles IV as was also the girded and ungirded gown. The paintings show us, however, for which class and in what surroundings it was thought proper to wear a cloak turned up above the forehead or pulled down over it. In joyful scenes the corner of the cloak is turned back; in scenes of grief it is pulled down over the forehead like the mourning scarf of the Virgin in the Crucifixion, Grief, Descent from the Cross.

As already mentioned above, the fashion of the period of Charles IV stabilised the types of the preceding period adding only a ceremonial character to them. Its contribution, as revealed by the works of art which have come down to us, must be sought elsewhere than in cut. It is shown in the extremely elaborate Italian materials adorned with the newest patterns, or in the reproduction of the folds of the fine Flanders cloth.

The school of the Master of Třeboň adhered to the portrayal of saints clad in plain cloth. However, not even this can hide the development and the changes which the Gothic ideal had slowly undergone. The figures become much heavier, the folds of the garments are no longer so dramatic. Instead the head-dress has become more elaborate, the S-shaped pose has lost its meaning, and the late Gothic detail, such as the sewn-on collar of the formerly simple cloak, finds its way into the pictures quite unintentionally as if to announce the end of the traditional fashion of the period of Charles IV.

32. CLOAK AND BELTS OF OLDER WOMEN
Detail with the Virgin and St. John.

Crucifixion from St. Barbara's Chapel near Třeboň, before 1400.
Tempera painting on pine wood, h. 125 cm., w. 95 cm.
Prague, National Gallery.

33. CLOAK WITH COLLAR
Detail with the figure of St. Margaret.

Painted frame of the Madonna Aracoeli, wood, width of the frame 11 cm.
School of the Master of the Třeboň Altar, about 1400. Prague, National Gallery.

34. TRADITIONAL CLOAK
Detail with the figure of St. Apollonia.

Painted frame of the Madonna Aracoeli, wood, width of the frame 11 cm.
School of the Master of the Třeboň Altar, about 1400. Prague, National Gallery.

81

The statue of the Virgin of Třeboň is a worthy representative of the end of the period. The statue is one of the many beautiful sculptures of the Virgin made in Bohemia about 1390. All the tendencies of the Gothic fashion sketched above from paintings are emphasised by the sculptor, who concealed the S-shaped pose by solid folds and created a harmonious whole. It incorporated the ideal from the close of the century, an ideal which is timeless. Even as far as proportions are concerned the ideal of antique beauty, with the head being one eighth of the body, is strictly observed.

The Virgin of Třeboň is dressed in a gown, of which only the border of the neckline and a corner peeping out between the folds at the bottom are visible (later filled in with a pattern). On the head she has a veil with a low almost worldly head-band. The veil (polychromed much later) falls in small cascades down to the bust, and reveals a girl's elaborate head-dress. Over the gown she wears a cloak made of a number of straight strips of cloth. The cloak tightly embraces the shoulders, forming moderate folds at the waist, draped at the left side and extending downwards into large, bowl-like folds. The corner of the left part of the cloak is held lifted by the right hand. At the right side the cloak is wound around the hand and here, too, it forms a small corner. All the draping described here, its beauty when held lifted, is justified by the sculptor's observations; he either arranged the drapery himself or impressed it on his memory by observing reality.

35.

The Madonna of Třeboň, about 1390.

Stone statue, height 124 cm.
Polychrome of a later time.
Třeboň, St. Giles Church.

The reason why we have devoted so much space to the draping and corners of the cloak is that it is customary to regard these as introduced by the artist to give style and not as realistic elements. The technical and functional analysis of the garments shows, however, that the artist took these details from reality. The elaborate drapery of the cloak and the close-fitting cut of the gown is a Gothic contrast emphasised by the material used for the two different garments. We have already mentioned the Flanders cloth which embraces the figure and the three dimensionality of the drapery catching the light and creating deep shadows. The Gothic period used this natural quality of the newly introduced material for its own purposes. "The body is concealed by the multitude of folds," — which is the basic aim of the Gothic style — "but the human being underneath seems to be full of dignity and nobly untouchable" (Gutmann). In the Middle Ages the material mainly chosen for the cloak of the Virgin Mary is plain and fine cloth. The weight and playful abundancy of folds indicate heavenly sweetness or the eternal destiny of the figure while maintaining close contact with reality.

36.

DETAIL OF THE CLASP FROM THE GARMENT OF ST. WENCESLAS

Triptych with the Madonna, St. Wenceslas and St. Palmatius. Tommaso da Modena. Italian school, 1357—67. Tempera painting on wood.

Karlštejn, Chapel of the Holy Cross.

37. COUVRE-CHEF WITH WIMPLE AND CAP-LIKE ARRANGEMENT

Detail from the Crucifixion. Unknown master of the circle of the Court school of painters, of Prague, about 1365. Mural painting on the front of the altar in the Chapel of St. Catherine at Karlštejn (cp. 45).

The Gothic line of the figure is usually crowned by an elaborate hairdress, which, however, only unmarried girls could have. The flowing hair, artificially waved and loosened, reflects the striving for formality of Gothic fashion. At the beginning of the Gothic period the hair falls down over the shoulders to the waist. Later the hairdress becomes wider above the ears, where the hair is either curled or put under the net. The Gothic lady as represented in our illustrations by princesses, saints or even the Virgin herself, adorned her hairdress with small crowns, while young girls wore a head-band and wreath; this is proved by prohibitions issued against both, as for instance in Perugia in the first half of the 14th century. In Perugia the authorities sought to uproot the habit of wearing crowns and wreaths, and not only of those made of gold and silver but also of those made of silk and painted paper; but of course fashion will be fashion and women women.

VIII. Madonna of Rome, about 1360.

39.

TYPICAL LINE OF GOTHIC DRESS
Detail with the Virgin.

Whole-page illumination on f. 55 showing the Annunciation.
Illuminated manuscript, Laus Mariae Konrad of Haimburk, called Mariale, about 1364.
Prague, Library of the National Museum, sign. XVI D 13.

91

40.

HEADBAND, VEIL AND HAIRDRESS
Detail of the initial O from the Adoration of the Magi, f. 97.
Liber viaticus, before 1364.

The manuscript was written for the Bishop of Litomyšl, Jan of Středa, as a pocket breviary.
Prague, Library of the National Museum, XIII A 12.

IX.

HEADBAND WITH CROWN AND VEIL AND HOODED MANTLE
Madonna of Veveří, about 1350.

Tempera painting on pine wood, h. 79 cm., w. 63 cm.
Comes from the Chapel of the Assumption in the churchyard near the Castle of Veveří in Moravia.
Prague, National Gallery.

41.

VEIL-LIKE WIMPLE

Detail with the Sacrifice in the Temple on f. 209. Liber viaticus, before 1364. Cp. no. 40.
Prague, Library of the National Museum.

42. VEIL WITH BLACK BORDER

Detail of Mary Magdalena, from the Crucifixion. Tempera painting on wood, h. 95 cm., w. 85.5 cm.

Master of Vyšší Brod. About 1350. Cp. no. II.
Prague, National Gallery.

42.

X. CLOAK PULLED UP TO COVER THE HEAD

Crucifixion, about 1350. Master of Vyšší Brod. Cp. supplement II.

43.

ARRANGEMENT OF THE HEAD-DRESS OF AN OLDER WOMAN;
VEIL, HEADBAND AND WIMPLE

Whole-page illumination on f. 34, Purification of the Virgin. Illuminated manuscript.

Laus Mariae Konrad of Haimburk, about 1364. (Cp. no. 39.)
Prague, Library of the National Museum, sign. XVI D 13.

44.

CLOAK DRAWN OVER THE HEAD WITH SHAWL-LIKE WHITE
COUVRE-CHEF

Detail with the figure of the Virgin.

Crucifixion from Vyšší Brod, before 1400.
Tempera painting on oak, h. 129.5 cm., w. 98 cm.
Prague, National Gallery.

XI.

Detail of the Entombment of Christ.
Master of the Třeboň Altar, about 1380.
Cp. no. VII.

45.

DETAIL OF THE GARMENT WITH PLASTICALLY APPLIED PATTERN

St. Barbara. Between 1357 and 1367. Master Theodoric.
Karlštejn, Chapel of the Holy Cross.

The Castle of Karlštejn was built in 1348 by Emperor Charles IV as the treasury of the imperial crown jewels; it occupies both on account of the reason why it was built and on account of its decoration a special position among European medieval castles; most of the decorations are found in the private chapels. The most interesting is the uniform decoration of the Chapel of the Holy Cross, the walls of which are inlaid with semiprecious stones, golden stuccos and a cycle of 127 panels with half-figures of saints, angels and prophets, which form together with the architecture one indivisible whole.

46.

Portrait of Anna Svídnická, the third wife of Emperor Charles IV.
Sandstone with remnants of old polychrome, about 1380.

Part of a portrait cycle of 21 busts in the triforium of the Cathedral of St. Vitus in Prague.
The cycle was probably made by order of Charles IV. The busts were made in the workshop known as the Hut of St. Vitus, under Peter Parler, the second masterbuilder and sculptor of the cathedral.

47.

Portrait of Johanna the Bavarian, the first wife of Wenceslas IV, died 1386.

Sandstone. Cp. no. 46.
Placed at the western side of the part of the St. Vitus triforium which is above the Chapel of St. John of Nepomuk, south of the polygonal end of the choir in the St. Vitus Cathedral in Prague.

48.

Portrait of Elisabeth Přemyslovna, the wife of John of Luxembourg, died 1330.

Sandstone. Cp. no. 46.
The portrait was made between 1375 and 1378, and is thus a posthumous portrait, while the other busts are portraits of living persons.

In the gallery of the triforium in the Cathedral of St. Vitus in Prague.

49.

DETAIL OF THE GARMENT OF A BISHOP WITH PLASTICALLY APPLIED PATTERN OF A STYLISED LOTUS

Master Theodoric. Cp. no. 45.

The panel is the last in the lower row of the left wall of the window recess in the Chapel of the Holy Cross at Karlštejn.

50.

Portrait of Blanche of Valois, the first wife of Charles IV.

Sandstone. Cp. no. 46.
On the south side of the triforium above the Chapel of St. John the Baptist, north of the polygonal end of the choir in the Cathedral of St. Vitus in Prague.

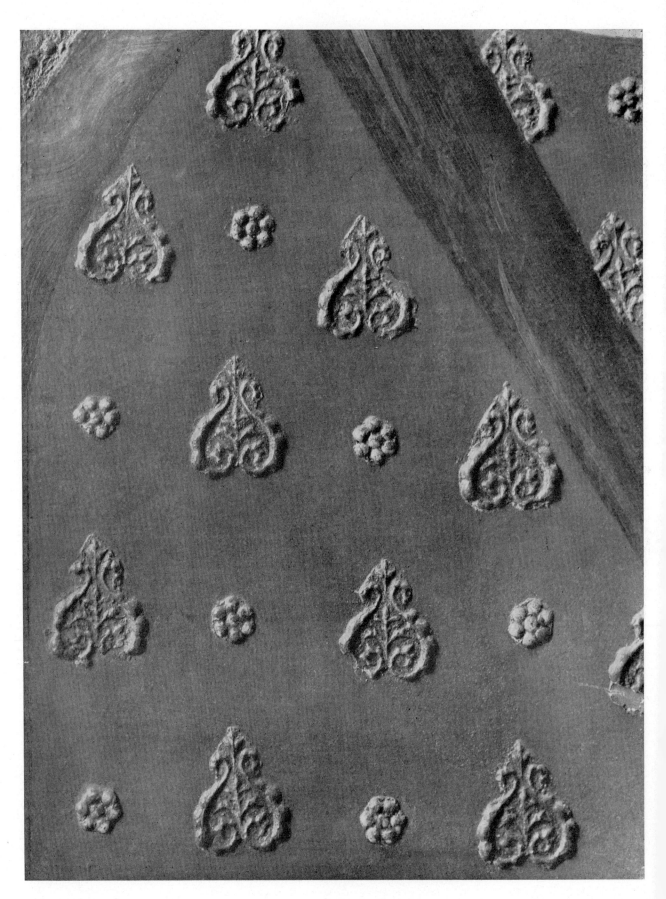

46.

47.

48.

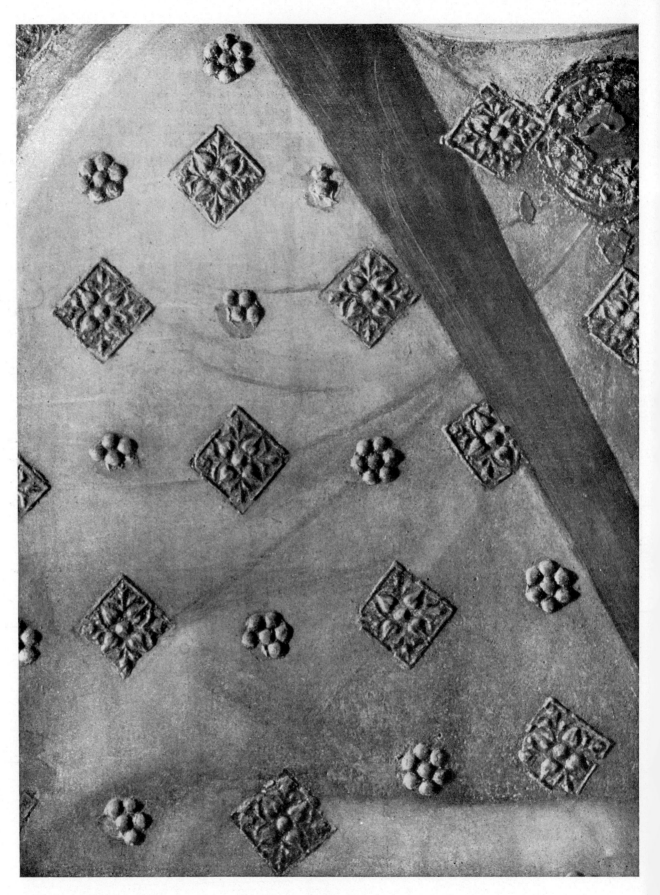

As is well known the first beginning of the Renaissance north of the Alps shows itself in the triforium in the St. Vitus Cathedral in Prague. Here we have a portrait gallery, so to speak, of the kings and queens of Bohemia and the architects and master builders of the Cathedral. Let us look a little closer at it. Anna Svídnická (1375-78) from the triforium has a hairdress which shows her adorable little nose to the greatest advantage. It is the same type of hairdress as the one which the painter has given St. Catharine of Budějovice. Blanche of Valois (1375-78), the first wife of Charles IV, has the same looped plaits and crown as the Master of Třeboň gave St. Margaret. Joan of Bavaria (1375-78), the first wife of Wenceslas IV, wears a rather archaic hairdress. With loosely hanging hair she wears a somewhat shorter veil, which peeps out from under the crown and is adorned with zig-zag motifs. The mother of Charles IV, Elisabeth Přemyslovna (1375-78), an old lady with arched forehead, has a high wimple with a tiny border and a closely fitting veil, falling down over the shoulders. Not one single hair escapes from under the tight almost nun-like couvre-chef, which is, however, in strong contrast to the benevolent smile of the matron. It is in fact the same type of veil as that we have seen on young ladies of the first half of the 14th century. The heaped up and high veils which belonged to the first eccentricities of Gothic fashion had already by the second half of the 14th century become simpler and were probably worn only by older women.

Our observations indicate that the queens who came from France are not more fashionably dressed than are the saints. The other women of the St. Vitus triforium, as for example Joan of Bavaria, are by far not so fashionably dressed as the Virgin in some of the paintings.

51.

DETAIL OF THE MATERIAL FROM THE GARMENT OF ST. OTTILIA (?)
WITH A PLASTICALLY APPLIED PATTERN OF SQUARES PLACED
SLANTINGLY, AND WITH CLASP

Tempera painting on wood. Master Theodoric. Cp. no. 45.
Middle panel of the upper row on the right side of the window recess behind the Epistle side of the altar
of the Chapel of the Holy Cross at Karlštejn.

52.

53.

52.

HOOD-LIKE CLOAK WITH VEIL
Detail of the painting of the Madonna of St. Vitus, about 1400.
Tempera painting on wood, 51 × 39.5 cm.

The painting was probably made for the St. Vitus Cathedral in Prague; in the fifties of the 19th century amethysts were set in the halo (the picture here shown has no amethysts as these were removed at the modern restoration).

Prague, National Gallery.

53.

HOOD-LIKE CLOAK WITH VEIL
Detail of the painting The Madonna of Zlatá Koruna, about 1410.
Tempera painting on wood, 68.5 × 50 cm.

The painting was probably made for the Cistercian monastery at Zlatá Koruna, founded by Přemysl Otakar II in 1263. In the 14th century, when the panel was ordered, the monastery of the Cistercians represented a powerful stronghold of the might of the Church; originally it was a symbol of the royal power over against the power of the nobility represented in southern Bohemia by the Rožmberks.

Today the picture is in the National Gallery in Prague.

54.

MODERN HAIRDRESS, WIMPLE AND VEIL OF ST. HELENA
AND HER SERVANT
Detail from the painting Finding and Testing of the Holy Cross, before 1420.
Tempera painting on spruce, 96 × 60 cm., apparently by a Moravian master.

Part of six pictures of a Passion cycle and of the Legend of the Holy Cross, from the Rajhrad Altar.
In the 19th century all 6 paintings were deposited in the Benedictine monastery of Rajhrad in Moravia, whence the name of the master has been derived.

Brno, Moravian Museum.

55.

DETAIL OF THE PATTERNED MATERIAL FROM THE GARMENT
OF THE MADONNA WITH CHRIST CHILD

Cp. no. 36.
Middle part of the triptych with Madonna, St. Wenceslas and St. Palmatius.
Italian School of 1357 - 1367.

Tempera painting on wood.
The painting was ordered in Italy by Charles IV on the occasion of his coronation and placed in the middle of the
wall above the sanctuary of the Chapel of the Holy Gross at Karlštejn.

XII.

BROCADES, EMBROIDERIES AND PATTERNS PAINTED
ON THE MATERIAL

Detail from the Madonna of Kladsko, about 1350.

Tempera painting on poplar, 186×95 cm.
Centre of the lost altar, given by the first Arch bishop of Prague, Ernest of Pardubice (figured on the panel
as donor) to the Augustinian monastery in Kladsko. Hence the name of the painting.

Berlin. Deutsches Museum.

116

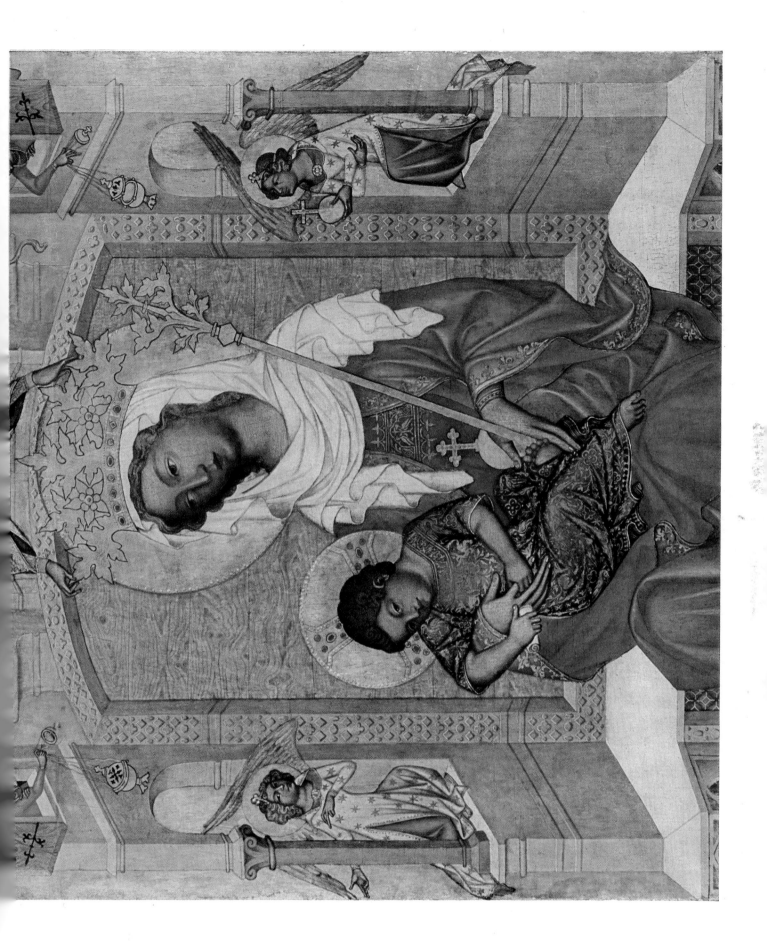

The greatness of the period of Charles IV shows itself both in the whole attitude to contemporary art as well as in the smallest detail of fashion, such as the finishing-off of sleeves, neckline or waist.

The plain, firm border of the early medieval period disappeared to give place to fringes (cp. the Madonna of Most and the Madonna of Strahov). Although fringes were used already in Antiquity it is characteristic for the Gothic period that they became one of its most beloved motifs.

In the works of art preserved from the time of Charles IV we do not any longer find long sleeves falling to the ground, with tippets and other forms of this fashionable motif typical of Gothic costume. The Gothic painter of this period paints only elaborate ceremonial garments, under which we only catch a glimpse of the sleeve of the kirtle and the finishing of the neckline, but instead we have more variations of the plain close-fitting sleeves.

56.

DETAIL OF THE SLEEVE WITH DECORATED CUFF FROM
THE STRAHOV MADONNA

Bohemian master of about 1350.

Tempera on wood, 94 × 84 cm.

Formerly the property of the Premonstratensian monastery of Strahov in Prague.
Prague, National Gallery.

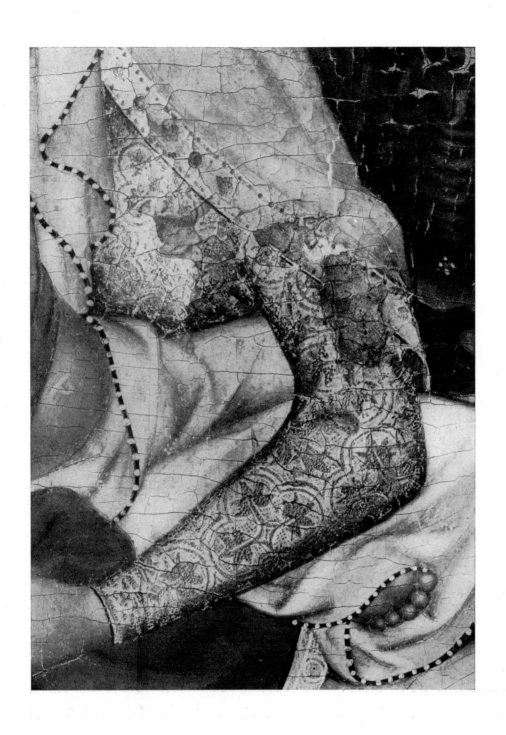

57.

DETAIL OF THE SLEEVE OF BROCADE OF THE MADONNA FROM
THE BIRTH OF CHRIST

Master of Vyšší Brod. Cp. no. 25 and suppl. V.

58. SLEEVE WITH ORNAMENTAL CUFF. DETAIL OF THE
MADONNA OF MOST
Cp. no. XIII.

XIII.

The Madonna of Most, before 1350.

Tempera painting on poplar, 53 × 40 cm.
Since 1578 in the West Bohemian church of the Capuchin monastery at Most.

There is also much more variety of material, although of course it would be worse than superfluous to add elaborate cuffs or a border to the precious brocade shown for example by the Master of Vyšší Brod. However, when the Master of Vyšší Brod took over the design of five-petalled flowers in round medallions from the half-woollen materials of Regensburg he adorned them with a double layer of gold (Hurníková). The golden cuffs of the Virgin of Most well match the dark, discreetly patterned silk of her gown. Again we find the municipality of Florence issuing prohibitions against the wearing of such costly cuffs (13th century) (cp. Floerke). The flowers in the pattern on the robe of the child are now freely scattered over the whole surface and avoid casting any deep shadows. The painting is thus made in a way which is diametrically opposed to that of the other Bohemian painters of the time.

The painters, however, who followed a more realistic trend in their art, as for instance the pupil of the Master of Třeboň or the painter of the panel at Hluboká, or even sometimes Master Theodoric, preferred cloth with close-fitting sleeves without any adornment. The uncovered part of the hand is fine and strikingly delicate even when painted by such an uncompromising realist as Theodoric.

59. CUTTING AND DECORATION (BUTTONS AND BELT) OF A GOTHIC
DRESS FROM THE MIDDLE OF THE 14th CENTURY

Detail, the figure of the angel and the three Maries; from the Ressurrection, about 1350.

Master of Vyšší Brod. (Cp. sup. III and no. 22.)

60. DETAIL OF GARMENT AND SIMPLE SLEEVE OF AN APOSTLE FROM
THE DESCENT OF THE HOLY GHOST

Cp. suppl. II.

61. Detail: Madonna with St. Bartholomew and St. Margaret, about 1400. Tempera painting on wood, 110 × 125.
Originally painted perhaps for the church at Krumlov in Southern Bohemia, later transferred to the South
Bohemian Neo-Gothic Castle of Hluboká.

62. DETAIL OF A SIMPLE SLEEVE

from the painting of St. Hedwig by master Theodoric. Cp. no. 45. Right marginal panel in the lower row on the
left side of the window recess in the south wall of the Chapel of the Holy Cross at Karlštejn.

127

61.

63. DETAIL OF THE GARMENT OF ST. CATHERINE WITH PARTLY
PLASTICALLY APPLIED PATTERN OF THE MATERIAL

Master Theodoric. Cp. suppl. XIV.

XIV.

Painting of St. Catherine.

Tempera painting on wood, 114.5 × 87 cm. Master Theodoric.
Cp. no. 45. Extreme right panel of the upper row on the right side of the window recess in the south wall of the
Chapel of the Holy Cross at Karlštejn.

A real contrast to the Master of Vyšší Brod is given by the second of the three outstanding painters of the Bohemian Gothic, Master Theodoric. He is principally known for the cycle of 127 panels with half figures of saints in the chapel of the Holy Cross at Karlštejn (about 1360). In these pictures, which belong to the most mysterious works of art of the Middle Ages, the painter deviated from the preceding as well as from the contemporary period both in his manner of painting and in the fashion he presented. The garments covering the figures were painted separately and in several variations. Faces and hands were added later. This method was chosen probably on account of the vastness of the task undertaken. The design was stencilled, and various shades of colour were used. The plasticity of the folds was achieved by means of shading with azure painted on top of the flat pattern. These transparent coats of paint indicated at the same time — in some instances at any rate — which kind of material it was, such as brocade for instance.

Not even Theodoric himself totally disregarded the fashionable way of painting of his time, and he, too, used plastic golden adornment for borders, gloves and mitres. They give the impression of applications of another material, especially at a short distance. These paintings, however, were meant to be looked at from afar.

The cycle of Vyšší Brod presents fragile figures clad in fashionable dresses, the colours of which form a harmonious whole, still further enhanced by the beautiful ornaments, and the whole cycle is painted with a delicacy which makes it reminiscent of the finest goldsmith's work. Compared with the cycle of Vyšší Brod Theodoric's painting as a whole and in its details appears coarse. But this is only so because Theodoric presented a different kind of monumentality, and also because the position of his painting high up on the walls of the chapel makes them look more like mural paintings than like paintings on wood. Further, when stamping is used for ornaments in painting the result will necessarily be coarser than when the ornaments are painted by hand.

The interesting point is here that the design of the Master of Vyšší Brod (belt of the angel in the Resurrection) and those of Theodoric are essentially of the same type and have the same ornamental motifs of the stamps as the border on the collar of St. Stephen in the cycle of Karlštejn. The rhomboid design here is the usual one for ornamentations of borders, and became a general European fashion, which, however, had developed independently in the different countries, although Cologne must be said to be the centre of the development of naturalistic designs of borders (Hurníková).

The motif which is most used in the cycle is that of the lotus flower; in the cycle, however, this motif has become so stylised and simplified that it would be difficult to find an analogy to it from that century. The pattern of material in the painting of St. Margaret seems to be the one which is relatively closest to the textile ornamentation of the 14th century; here the lotus has preserved the stylised pointed form of the Gothic period. Above this pattern we have the stamped plastic ornamentation transforming the basic design.

64. THE GARMENT WITH STYLISED PLANT ORNAMENT

Detail of the garment of St. Vitus. Master Theodoric.

Tempera painting on wood, 114×93 cm. Prague National Gallery.

65. DETAIL OF THE PLASTIC AND PAINTED PATTERN
OF THE GARMENT OF ST. AGNES

Master Theodoric. Cp. no. 45.

First left panel in the upper row on the left wall of the window recess in the south wall of the Chapel
of the Holy Cross at Karlštejn.

66—67.

DETAIL OF THE GARMENT OF ST. STEPHEN WITH PLASTICALLY
APPLIED BORDER TERMINATING THE SLEEVES
Master Theodoric. Cp. no. 45.

Extreme panel to the right of the lower row on the right wall of the window recess in the north wall of the Chapel
of the Holy Cross at Karlštejn.

136

67.

Almost all patterns of materials from the cycle of Karlštejn can be more or less derived from this basic motif shown on the garment of St. Margaret. Sometimes it lacks the plastic ornamentation and the oval motif. When this is so, the plastic ornamentation appears on the borders. Sometimes we find only the plastic ornamentation, but the lotus motif remains its basis. Probably the various combinations and variations of the lotus ornamentation arose from the desire to use decoration which could be fully appreciated even from afar. It is most interesting to notice that the neighbouring ribs of the vaulting continue into the picture, thus connecting the wall with the painting. The frame, wall and picture are stamped with the same stencils.

68. DETAIL OF THE COLLAR OF POPE CLEMENT (?)
Master Theodoric. Cp. no. 45.

First panel to the left of the second row from above on the entrance half-wall on the north side of the Chapel of the Holy Cross at Karlštejn.

69. DETAIL OF THE PLASTIC AND PAINTED PATTERN FROM THE GARMENT OF ST. MARGARET
Master Theodoric. Cp. no. 45.

Extreme right panel of the upper row on the left side of the window recess in the south wall of the Chapel of the Holy Cross at Karlštejn.

70. DETAIL OF THE DECORATION OF THE COLLAR FROM THE
PAINTING OF ST. AUGUSTINE

Master Theodoric. Cp. no. 45.

Lower panel on the south side of the wall of the window recess in the middle of the entrance wall of the Chapel
of the Holy Cross at Karlštejn.

71. DETAIL OF GARMENT AND PLASTICALLY APPLIED DECORATIONS
FROM THE PAINTING OF A BISHOP

Master Theodoric. Cp. no. 45.

Middle panel of the upper row on the right wall of the window recess in the north wall of the Chapel
of the Holy Ghost at Karlštejn.

71.

72. DETAIL OF THE MATERIAL AND DRESS DECORATION AND
JEWELLERY, FROM THE PAINTING OF A BISHOP
Master Theodoric. Cp. no. 45.

Extreme panel to the right of the upper row on the left wall of the window recess in the north wall of the Chapel
of the Holy Cross at Karlštejn.

The close relation between the ornamentation on the material in the paintings and the architectural details shows that the former has no relation to fashion as far as the reproduction of textiles in these paintings is concerned. The date of origin of this ornamentation, appearing here in
many variations, may be at least approximately estimated. Its basis is probably the motif of Venetian brocades of the 14th century (Falke, picture 416). The atomising of the motif, its simpli-
fication, misinterpretation, and wrong utilisation were the reasons why the pictures were dated
as late as the Renaissance by some historians. If, however, we take into consideration that the
Renaissance textile patterns grew in size and that the pomegranate motif gained in importance
in Renaissance ornamentation, we cannot imagine that Theodoric's lotus ornament even in its
most degenerate form can be later than the end of the Gothic period. Moreover as the same patterns are used in the Florentine and Tyrolese wall paintings of the 14th century and in Theodoric's

142

paintings we may take it as established that all belong to the same period — thus we have here an exquisite example of how similarity in details may help to settle a controversial question.

73. Detail of the jewellery on the garment of St. Palmatius from the middle part of the triptych: Madonna with St. Wenceslas and St. Palmatius.
Italian School of 1357 - 1367. Tommasso da Modena.

Tempera painting on wood. Cp. no. 55.
Karlštejn, Chapel of the Holy Cross, above the sanctuary in the middle of the altar wall.

The illustrations to the next chapter are taken from the Bible of Wenceslas IV. It is an unfinished illuminated Bible in six parts, in German, belonging to the group of manuscripts known as the Wenceslas manuscripts. The Bible was made for Wenceslas IV by the Master of the Royal Mint M. Rotlev, between 1390-1400. The Bible is richly illuminated with an intricate grape-vine motif, phantastic animals, allegorical and symbolic figures. Rotlev belonged to an old patrician family in Prague; the name means Red Lion and was taken from the house "At the Red Lion" (ad ruffum leonem). The Rotlevs' house on the corner of the Železná ulice was later acquired by Wenceslas IV, who gave it to the Charles University in 1383. The University re-named it the Carolinum in honour of her founder Charles IV, and it is as much the centre of the University today at is was at the time when the University in its hall elected Jan Hus as Rector of the University. The close relations between M. Rotlev and the king are proved not only by the series of heraldic designs on the Carolinum, but also by the ornamentation of the Rotlev Bible, which Rotlev had specially made for the king, and which shows an intimate knowledge of the particular taste of the king. The Bible is extremely richly decorated with symbols — kingfisher and bush, towel, pail and barbers. The book is deposited in Vienna in the State Library, sign. Codex 2759-2764.

74.

Humorous motif showing Wenceslas IV. and bathkeeper in stocks.

FASHION DURING THE PERIOD OF WENCESLAS IV

Compared with the ceremonial and traditional character of the fashion of the period of Charles IV the fashion of the following period appears more revolutionary, especially in style. It is the style at its fullest development and furthest removed from its beginning. The period has retained the love of splendour in the choice of material as far as court circles are concerned. But it has a greater choice of garments both for the various classes as well as for everyday use. It is during this period that we first meet with specific garments made for members of the various guilds, with specific garments for work, for social occasions etc. This period deprives the garment of its ceremonial character and secularises it. In the first place, and in full accordance with the spirit of the period, it emphasises the cut and form of the garment, adjusting it completely to the body. On this basis the period of Wenceslas IV created a fashion in Bohemia which we may call, together with the painting, sculpture and architecture of the period, "the beautiful fashion".

As we can speak in the history of the painting, sculpture and architecture of this period in Bohemia of the beautiful style, so we can also speak of it in the history of fashion. The Bohemian beautiful fashion divided the woman's figure in a new way, it used a new line, which for the first time emphasised the hips, breast and abdomen. This new line was probably introduced by Queen Isabella of France (1371—1435).

75-81. SIMPLE DRESSES OF THE PRAGUE BATHKEEPERS FROM THE END
OF THE 14th CENTURY

Ornamentation of grape-vine motif in the second volume of the Bible of Wenceslas IV.

In its country of origin this style was so eccentric as to be a constant source of ridicule and laughter. When, however, it was transplanted to Bohemia it underwent a change. Here it developed into one of the more attractive styles of that formalism with which the beautiful style veiled the realism of Gothic Bohemian art. There appeared costumes which belong to the most remarkable creations in the history of fashion.

While for the preceding period we had to go to more or less official or public works of art for our material, we now find that our material comes from works of art of a more private character, especially from manuscripts.

A series of Bibles made for the library of Wenceslas IV furnish us with some of our illustrations. The subject of the illuminations in these manuscripts are closely connected with the life of the king and his wife Sophie. This explains the substantial difference in themes, in the choice of figures, and in the way in which they are presented. Works of art of the former period showed us, for example, church dignitaries and royal persons on official ceremonial occasions. The Wenceslas fashion, introduced by the king himself — as in France it was Philip the Beautiful who personally initiated fashions towards the end of the 15th century — may also have church dignitaries and royal persons as the subject of a painting, but the scene presented is not a ceremonial occasion but is of a more private character. The manuscript, the personal property of the king, is filled with humorous comments, in the form of marginal illuminations, on the king's likes and dislikes.

In the works of art from the period of Charles IV we studied paintings of the Virgin and saints in which the figures were veiled in draped cloaks, and we compared them with the official portraits of princesses and queens. Now we must reverse this procedure. The richest source is for our purpose the garment of bathkeepers, with whom the man of the Middle Ages liked to spend his time.

The figure, formerly completely veiled, now gives place to a figure whose form shines through the drapery. Instead of the almost orientally splendid garments of heavy materials we have now light, transparent gowns. For votive paintings of the period of Charles IV representing the Virgin and saints we have now small illustrations to the Old and New Testament. The illuminator depicts in the biblical events the life he sees round him, he portrays in his drolleries the king and his wife Sophie, the latter is supposed to be the figure in the bathkeeper's garment (Schlosser).

For the period of Charles IV we lacked material about women's undergarment. We are now fully compensated for this. From the inexhaustible store of costumes shown in the manuscripts we have chosen a few types of garments which we shall use to explain the main characteristics of the Wenceslas fashion.

The basic line of this fashion is given by the transparent light garment of the bathkeepers. It is actually a sleeveless chemise, cut diagonally so as to emphasise the shape of waist and bust. In principle we might compare this type of garment with a summer dress or lingerie of the 20th century. In its higher form — we have in mind figures of bathkeepers dressed in long garments — these garments resemble strikingly evening dresses of the 20th century.

The bathkeepers wear garments of different length. The shortest garment, which reaches only to below the knee, is usually the plainest without any adornment, and it was probably worn by assistants — this may be inferred on the basis of analogy with men's fashion of the 14th century where the length of the cloak distinguished the nobleman from the commoner (Falke). The garment reaching to the calf probably indicated a higher social rank.

Sometimes the garment reaches down to the ground, and then it is most beautiful.

The basic pattern is not influenced by the length. The longest garment has a striking resemblance to the garments of the highest social strata of the time. The plainest type on the other hand is regarded as the basis of the working garment (Zíbrt).

82. NIGTHGARMENT WITH COUVRE-CHEF
Cp. no. 74.

Detail from the Birth of Samson on f. 34. From the second volume of the Bible of Wenceslas IV.

The neckline of this garments is always straight. The shoulder straps are pushed outward as far as possible, and they are either of the same or of a different material from the rest. This holds good also about the hem. The difference between the elaborate garment with a straight neckline and the garment with a deep cut neckline of the bathkeepers is simply that the bathkeeper's garments have no sleeves while the garments of the Gothic lady of the Wenceslas period always had long sleeves.

The belt of the bathkeeper's garment might vary very much. It is often indicated only by the cut (similarly as the elaborate garment), or it consists of a broad sash with fluttering ends. The most important new fashion is the narrowing in at the waist with the sash round the hips.

83. UNDERGARMENT AND NIGHTGARMENT FROM THE END
OF THE 14th CENTURY

Detail from the Birth of Samson, from the second volume of the Bible of Wenceslas IV, f. 17ʳ.

This division gives the garment of the Wenceslas period a new character. The fashion line is not determined by the length of the garment but by the placing of the waist. In this respect women's fashion of the period brings a most important new feature, which curiously enough no one has mentioned. In men's fashion, which in this period is even more important, this change took place already in the middle of the 14th century.

A special insignia of bathkeepers are girdles, usually blue, so that they contrast with the whiteness of their garments. Undoubtedly the girdle had some other, deeper meaning. During the Wenceslas period it became the adornment of all humorous miniatures, and together with the kingfisher it found its way into architectural ornamentation (cp. the Bridge Tower of the Charles Bridge in Prague). It was taken over into the guild insignia of bathkeepers. (This despised guild achieved the same status as other guilds under a privilege of Wenceslas IV of 1406.) The girdle is the simplest and the most expressive way of adorning and dividing a garment. It is the simplest because it helps to make the most important changes while the style remains the same, and it is the most expressive because its arrangement depends on the mood of the wearer.

84.

CLOSE FITTING DRESSES OF BATHKEEPERS, WITHOUT
SHOULDER STRAPS

Detail from the initial D, showing the king among bathkeepers, f. 174ʳ, from the first volume of the Bible
of Wenceslas IV.

85.

CLOSE FITTING DRESSES OF BATHKEEPERS WITH SHOULDER STRAPS AND WITH NETS OVER THE HAIR

Detail of the illuminated D showing bathkeepers and king.

From the Bible of Wenceslas IV.

Varied, too, are the head-dresses of the bathkeepers, probably arranged according to some unknown rule. The bathkeepers wear their hair long and flowing with wreaths or caps or crespines, with strips of material which sometimes conceal the hair or leaves it hanging loose. Hair tightly plaited into stiff pigtails over the ears are probably reserved for bathkeepers of the highest rank. The highest form of this head-dress is a kind of ducal cap, which probably had a deeper meaning in this still mysterious hierarchy of bathkeepers. Some of them have a bucket and a wisp of straw, some only a bucket. No matter how beautiful or plain their dress is, they all have bare feet and arms.

Let us now examine the material out of which this plain garment of the Wenceslas period was made. Usually the garment was probably made of a washable material. The simplest material is used for a well-cut garment completed by a sash, but the plainer the material the more it brings out the shape of the body. Although we find ourselves still in the Middle Ages, we are constantly reminded of the Renaissance attitude to the nude.

153

86. DRESS OF BATHKEEPERS DECORATED WITH FLUTTERING SASH,
NET COVERING THE HAIR

Details from the borders with bathkeepers, f. 57ʳ.

From the third volume of the Bible of Wenceslas IV.

We shall now compare the bathkeeper's garments with those of the higher social classes as we find them in the manuscripts of the period of Wenceslas IV.

In birth scenes of the preceding period the women in labour usually lie cloaked in beds adorned with the most splendid brocades. Reverence led the painter to paint the women always in elaborate garments. Now they are painted more realistically in a chemise, which has the same

87. A COMPLICATED HAIRDRESS FROM THE END OF THE 14th CENTURY
Detail of the borders with bathkeepers, f. 33.

From the second volume of the Bible of Wenceslas IV.

cut as the garment of bathkeepers with the same accessories, a round cap and plaits at the ears. The basis of women's night gowns is therefore the chemise — the garment of bathkeepers. A noble woman in labour, as for example the mother of Samson, wears the same garment as a bathkeeper of higher rank, adorned with dark shoulder straps, and it is distinguishable from the former by a modern couvre-chef only.

88. DRESS OF AN ELDERLY LADY FROM THE END
OF THE 14th CENTURY

Detail from Samson goes with his parents to Timnah, f. 18 of the second volume of the Bible
of Wenceslas IV.

The bathkeepers at work are illustrated by the illuminators of the Wenceslas Bibles, once
inset in the grape-vine motif and once in an initial. They are dressed in sleeveless garments, but
without any shoulder straps. The garment is very tight, and we must surmise that it was made
according to fashion.

We have now just one small step to the more elaborate garment. The bathkeepers shown are

89. CLOSE FITTING ELABORATE DRESSES WITH DEEPLY CUT-OUT
NECKLINE FROM THE END OF THE 14th CENTURY
Detail from Delilah and Samson, f. 20, from the second volume of the Bible
of Wenceslas IV.

probably not on duty. The garment is of a different, darker colour and has long sleeves. In principle it is an ungirded garment taken over from the first half of the 14th century. It is, however,
further developed in all details. It is the true precursor of the Italian elaborate garment from the
end of the 15th century. It was probably this kind of garment which provoked the Milanese
priest Casola in 1494 to ask the malicious question as to why the garment did not slip off.

90.

CLOSE FITTING HOLIDAY DRESS OF THE PRAGUE BATHKEEPERS,
WITH DEEPLY CUT-OUT NECKLINE

Bahtkeeper inset in grape-vine motive. From the second volume of the Bible of Wenceslas IV.

In Bohemia at the beginning of the 15th century a similar garment was worn by young girls and only slightly altered for married women. Delilah may serve as an example. On the head she has a veil arranged into a high point distinguishing her from unmarried girls. The same veil covers the throat, but under the veil may be seen a deep neckline not much smaller than that of the bathkeepers. In addition the neckline is emphasised by a hem in two colours. The garment with long sleeves and a very long skirt fits even tighter than that of the bathkeepers thanks to the plain but solid material out of which it was made. Below the bodice it forms deep horizontal folds modelling the abdomen, ending in long pointed corners at the feet. Delilah's dress is of course more provocative than that of the bathkeepers. It is worth observing that the deep cut of the neckline is not covered with patterned material.

Contrary to Delilah's dress, the garment of Samson's mother, who is presented as being elderly, is more traditional. The veil completely covers the neckline. The lifting of the garment, held up by the right hand, fashionable many years ago, is now old fashioned.

91.

SOCIETY CLOAK AND DRESSES WITH THE LATEST ACCESSORIES

The initial H from the manuscript of Willehalm de Orange, of 1387, the oldest Wenceslas manuscript.

Vienna, State Library (Cod. A. N.)

Similarly out of date is the garment of the ladies-in-waiting from the Golden Bull. It is only a timid precursor of the Wenceslas garment. The court ceremonial added wide sleeves extending down from the shoulders and furlined. The Queen herself is presented in a garment of heavy brocade closely fitting right up to the chin. She is veiled in this garment as in a cloak and does not bear the slightest resemblance to her daughter-in-law Sophie, who used to be dressed in the most tight-fitting and most low-cut garments, by which she distinguished herself from all the ladies-in-waiting. Not even on official occasions, as at her coronation on the 15th day of March, 1400, when she was, according to a contemporary description, clad in a ceremonial gown of an almost priestly type with golden sandals, did she observe medieval rules since she wore on her head a wreath of pearls (Stloukal).

All types of the Wenceslas garments are to be found in the miniature in the scene "Miriam the prophetess, the sister of Aaron, took a timbrel in her hand, and all the women went out with timbrels and with dances".

159

92.

DRESS OF THE PRAGUE BATHKEEPERS,
DECORATED WITH FLUTTERING SASH AT THE WAIST
AND SCARF OVER THE HEAD

Bathkeeper inset in grape-vine motive from the second volume of the Bible of Wenceslas IV.

93.

CEREMONIAL, ELEGANT DRESS FROM THE END OF THE 14th
CENTURY, WITH FLOWING SCARF AND WIDE SLEEVES
Detail from the Bulla Aurea Caroli IV regis.

Illuminated Latin manuscript, 1390 - 1400. It belonged to the library of Wenceslas IV.
Detail from an illumination showing the king, queen, and three women, f. 33.
Vienna, State Library, sign. Cod. 338.

94. PATTERNED DRESS OF BATHKEEPERS, WITH ALL
APPERTAINING DETAILS
The initial U with a bathkeeper, f. 108. From the second volume of the Bible of Wenceslas IV.

It is as if the painter of the miniature had wanted to present basic types of garments and couvre-chef of all classes and ages. As the last in the row walks a young girl in a garment which we may call a typical Wenceslas garment, with deep neckline and flowing hair. She is dressed in the same fashion as bathkeepers off duty.

The second figure, veiled in the traditional cloak pulled over the head (wrap), presents a some-what elderly woman who has taken a firm stand against the spirit of fashion.

95.

The initial U with a bathkeeper, f. 130.
From the first volume of the Bible of Wenceslas IV.

The third figure with a veil arranged in a point shows the cloak of a socially important woman. On her undergarment we notice interesting embroidered cuffs on the sleeves, extending crown-like towards the palms.

The fourth figure contrasts with the preceding one. She has an even deeper neckline than the bathkeepers, her garment has the same tight fit, but long sleeves which are completed with round fur shoulder straps. The silhouette is outlined by a round bonnet.

Not even the oldest and gravest of the women in this procession, the sister of Aaron, veiled in a plain wimple, has been spared by the striking modernisation. The fashionable eccentricity of her garment are the tippets of the sleeves, the transformed reminder of the loosely hanging ceremonial sleeves of ladies-in-waiting, which turned into very narrow flying bands emphasising the vertical line. Even here we are reminded of the flowing lines in the bathkeepers' knotted girdles. In addition to wreaths, veils and cloaks arranged into points we meet for the first time in the Bibles of Wenceslas IV with the hat. It is quite new and has had no precursors.

Fashion at the time of Wenceslas did not use the usual cones and horns with extended veils nor berets. In this respect it is original. The high-girdled garment was cut almost in Empire style and worn with a bonnet. This special kind of hat is known as *boemische kogeln*. It is one of the details of the Wenceslas' fashion which made their appearance first in Bohemia, and which spread to the whole of Central Europe.

The basic style of the tight-fitting garment becomes more elaborate. It has buttons from the neckline down to the knees. Thus the vertical line is emphasised by a new detail, which since then has remained a part of women's garments. Even the sleeves, formerly very simple, cover almost the whole of the palm and spread out fan-wise over the knuckles.

The two details of buttons and furs were taken over by the Wenceslas fashion from the preceding period. Buttons on garments appear for the first time about the middle of the 14th century, when the garment continued to get tighter and tighter until it fitted like a glove. It was then that the cloak became a dress, and the toga definitely a thing of the past (Falke).

Fondness for furs grew in the Wenceslas period to such an extent that even close-fitting garments were trimmed with fur at the shoulders, and in addition were completed by a fur cap. The cloaks sewn on to the garment give the impression of wings.

In that period of new fashions a new dramatic occurrence in the development of women's clothes took place when the garment was divided into a bodice, skirt, and short coat. The most important factor is here the surcoat, which we know already from the Velislav Bible, and which was taken up again by the Wenceslas period. The surcoat helped to emphasise important parts of the woman's body, the neckline and the hips. It is a precursor of the short coat. It divided and emphasised by its cut and embroidery the slimness of the waist, the broadness of the hips, and the modelling of the bust. From the surcoat, embroidered with pearls and made of different materials, the development of the Gothic garment had no more a long way to go to reach the final phase when bodice became divided from skirt. It became an independent part of dress provided with pockets. This formed the culmination and end of the development of the fashion of the Wenceslas period.

96. DRESS OF BATHKEEPERS WITH SASH ON THE HIPS,
CAP AND LOOSENED HAIR
The initial U with bathkeepers, f. 112.

From the third volume of the Bible of Wenceslas IV.

96.

97.

97—98. SERIES OF THE MOST DIFFERENT ELABORATE DRESSES FROM
THE END OF THE 14th CENTURY

The illumination showing Mary, sister of Aaron, with women, f. 69.

From Exodus, in the Bible of Wenceslas IV.

98.

The second, truly revolutionary new fashion is the lowering of the waist down to the hips, which disturbed the basic vertical character of Gothic fashion.

This change has not received the attention it deserves, its importance may approximately be compared with the introduction of horizontal division in architure; in Bohemia this style was introduced by Petr Parléř in the building of the St. Vitus Cathedral in Prague.

99. CLOSELY FITTING, BUTTONED DRESSES MADE AFTER THE LATEST
FASHION OF THE 14th CENTURY

Detail of illumination from the manuscript of Willehalm de Orange of 1387. Vienna, State Library (cod. A. N.).

100. SAMPLE OF GOTHIC BROCADE

Detail of the cover of the Death of the Virgin. From the altar at Roudnice, about 1410. Tempera painting on wood, 147 × 118.5 cm. The altar was painted probably for the church of the Virgin at Roudnice.

Prague, National Gallery.

100.

For the first time the horizontal line is emphasised, and it interrupted the garment twice, once by the neckline forming an oval and framing the shoulders, stressed by fur, and a second time by the girdle at the hips. This division of the garment indicates a Renaissance tendency. The girdle moved down to the hips is a rather rare phenomenon in the history of fashion, although it is repeated as late as in the sixties of the 19th century and twice in the 20th century; it may be ascribed to a change in opinion as to what constitutes the beauty of a woman's figure. The line thus given is indicated best by the simple garments of the royal bathkeepers, which exaggerated all the elements of fashion. The garment remained tight-fitting, thus indicating not the trend of future fashion but the future ideal of a woman's figure.

Now we still have to take up the problem of the cloak. In the preceding periods it was the most important garment, now it was being deprived of its importance. Little attention was devoted to its portrayal, probably because it did not reveal but concealed the outline of the figure. Notwithstanding this fact a substantial change occurred in its development.

In the preceding period we had cloaks which still were an echo of antique fashion. The cloak of the Wenceslas period resembles the modern cloak. It is free of all folds and lost its connection

102.

with the wrap and toga. The long cloak of the Wenceslas period is open in front and furlined. Like the garment and cap it is trimmed with fur, which is used for borders even on the ceremonial outer garment. This trimming, originally only meant to be a protection against the cold and therefore not visible, was recognised by the Wenceslas period as more suitable for public occasions than gold and precious stones, which remained on the garments of the preceding period as a reminder of the somewhat barbarous overestimation of material. Thus the Wenceslas period showed not only a better taste but also a sense for function and laid one of the foundations of present fashion.

The cloak of the Wenceslas period, cut in the same way as the garment and furlined at the neck, was usually completed with a fur cap framing the face. The women of the highest nobility wore in addition a crown. The cover of the cloak was very often of brocade, the lining, according to many records was made of fur (Zíbrt). Thus the antique toga changed into the medieval cloak, finally to become the Central European furcoat. It is no longer reminiscent of the antique culture which flourished in the warm Mediterranean climate. This is one of the realistic characters of the Wenceslas fashion, which changed materials and styles, adjusting them to climate.

103.

ELABORATE DRESS DECORATED WITH FUR
The initial D from the manuscript of Willehalm de Orange, of 1387 (Cp. no. 91).

In the Wenceslas period Bohemian fashion reached its climax. In its too great refinement it carried the seeds of its own decay. The fundamental change, which occurred at the beginning of the 15th century, was caused not only by the death of Wenceslas IV, whose court was of great importance for Bohemian fashion, and during whose reign it reached its climax, but by the following political, economic and social changes. The Hussite people's revolution brought to a sudden stop the existing development of fashion and brought about a basic change both in men's and women's garments of the Hussite period. This is in strong contrast to the development in England, where neither the peasant's revolt nor Lollardism became national movements, influencing the whole of the life of the community.

104.

ELABORATE DRESS WITH CUFFS OVER THE HANDS
The initial R from the manuscript of Willehalm de Orange, of 1387.

The working garment was most typical of the fashion; it was freed from all court refine-
ments, and became in Bohemia a kind of mirror of the time. The works of art of the period which
reflect this new fashion have changed substantially. It is not necessary to compare them with the
Italian Cinquecento, for which handbooks on fashion show the garments. But we must turn our
attention to illuminated manuscripts, breviaries, Bibles and calendars. These show no longer any
interest in court circles but in the people. The late illuminated manuscripts as well as the early
printed books show us the fashion of various classes and professions of medieval Bohemian society,
whose revolt opened the world movement of the Reformation, and who carried through the first
social revolution.

The garment of the midwife, an elderly and worthy woman, often portrayed in the 14th and 15th centuries in miniatures and paintings on wood in birth scenes is almost the same in the middle of the 14th century as at the end of the 15th century. It is loose, chemise-like with sleeves rolled up to the elbow. In the Velislav Bible the midwife wears in addition a cloak, a kind of cloak falling loosely down to the ground, and which has been preserved up to the present day in the ordinary peasant garment.

The actual insignia of the class is the couvre-chef, which remained almost unchanged for 150 years. It is combined with a kind of head-band with which it forms an elaborate wimple, framing the face and covering the hair.

105.

WHAT RULES APPLIED IN SITTING FOR SOCIETY AT THE END OF THE MIDDLE AGES

Detail of the illumination showing Anna, wife of Elcanus, pouring out wine, f. 33, from the second volume of the Bible of Wenceslas IV.

106.

MODERN PROPORTIONS AND POSES FROM THE END
OF THE MIDDLE AGES

Detail of the illumination of the Bethlehem woman leaving her husband, f. 24, from the second volume
of the Bible of Wenceslas IV.

175

107.

TOWN DRESSES AND CLOAKS FROM THE SECOND HALF
OF THE 14th CENTURY

Illumination showing virgins vowing perpetual chastity, f. 45 v.
Tomáš Štítný: Six treatises on common Christian matters, of 1376.

Prague, National and University Library, sign. XVII A. 6.

A similar wimple with a zig-zag finishing (piping) may be seen on the midwife in the birth scene from the cycle of the Master of Vyšší Brod (about 1350). This figure was undoubtedly repainted later.

The midwife's loose garment shows a basic change. The bodice separated from the skirt is new; it has acquired its final form in the period of Wenceslas IV. Today it is impossible to decide whether it was the elaborate garment which for the first time carried out this basic change, or whether it was the working garment, for which this new division is most convenient. It is however certain that this separation of skirt from bodice, called "robe", occurred in Bohemia as elsewhere in the 15th century (Falke). Therefore the garment of the woman preparing the bath in the birth scene of the Master of Vyšší Brod could not have been made in the 14th century.

108.

DRESS WITH LIRIPIPE, BUTTONS AND GIRDLE ON THE HIPS

Detail of an illuminated manuscript with the figure of the courtisane, f. 37.

Tomáš Štítný: Six treatises on common Christian matters, of 1376.

Prague, National and University Library, sign. XVII A. 6.

109.

DRESS WITH FUR AND GIRDLE AT THE HIP
Detail of the illumination Death of Athalia, f. 169.
From the second volume of the Bible of Wenceslas IV.

110. TOWN DRESSES WITH BUTTONS
Detail of Women receiving David, f. 56.
From the second volume of the Bible of Wenceslas IV.

111. DRESS WITH SURCOAT EMPHASISING IN A NEW WAY
THE MEDIEVAL S-SHAPED POSE
Detail from the Sacrifice of Samuel, f. 34, from the second volume of the Bible of Wenceslas IV.

112. DRESS WITH SURCOAT
Detail of the illumination showing Thamar and Amon, f. 89, from the second volume of the Bible
of Wenceslas IV.

179

III.

112.

113.

SUMPTUOUS DRESS DECORATED WITH PEARLS AND FUR,
FROM THE END OF THE 14th CENTURY

Details of an illumination of an angel announcing to Manoah and his wife the birth of Samson,
f. 17, from the second volume of the Bible of Wenceslas IV.

114.

DRESS WITH SURCOAT AND LIRIPIPE
Detail of illumination of the Wenceslas Bibel.

We find in the Bibles of Wenceslas IV the same garment worn by midwives. It appears that besides the garment of bathkeepers this was one of the first guild garments which became a costume no longer subject to changing fashion. (A number of baroque portraits confirms this assumption.)

115.

CEREMONIAL ROYAL CLOAKS, FROM THE END OF THE 14th CENTURY
Detail of the initial D of the manuscript of Willehalm de Orange, of 1387.

The figure of the midwife from the birth scene is painted in an almost standard manner, but the changes in the ornamentation on the bed-linen, which is an indispensable supplement of this scene, are remarkable. In the 14th century we find for example sheets embroidered with a meander pattern (Liber viaticus). At the beginning of the 15th century among the post-Hussite works of art sheets are adorned with a type of folk embroidery consisting of circles, dots and tendrils arranged

116.

CEREMONIAL ROYAL CLOAKS, WITH CAP AND "BOEMISH KOGEL"
FROM THE END OF THE 14th CENTURY
Detail of the initial D of the manuscript of Willehalm de Orange, of 1387.

in wide stripes. The ornamentation appears to be embroidered on the linen. The first specimen
of woven checkered bed-linen comes from the eighties of the 15th century, although the woven
checkered pattern is almost certainly of a much earlier date, just as it has kept itself as a favoured
general European pattern to this day.

117.

Detail with Queen Sophia, the wife of Wenceslas IV, enthroned.
From the second volume of the Bible of Wenceslas IV.

The town woman's garment was close-fitting, and in line it is not inferior to the elaborate garment. The veils of city women adjusted themselves to modern arrangement so that they either formed broad corners above the ears, or they were ornamentally finished off by an artificial curling imitating hairdress. In the 15th century the town garment developed in its own way due to the improved social conditions of the town population. The scarf-wrap and apron are two distinguishing marks which appeared at the beginning of the 15th century as indispensable attributes of the garment of the working woman.

The country woman working in the fields wore a veil and also an apron, tied over her loose garment with sleeves.

It is a garment which has been preserved almost unchanged to this day.

We find it almost unchanged in Bohemian calendars from the beginning of the 15th century. This time without an apron, but with large tippets at the sleeves.

The garment of working women from the Olomouc Bible (first quarter of the 15th century) is still loose and comfortable, thus fulfilling the basic requirements of garments for those doing fieldwork. It is, however, girded at the hips, probably under the influence of the Wenceslas fashion, which moved the waistline downwards.

This change, which originally was used to emphasise the figure, is out of place here. In general it may be said that any similar mechanical adoption of fashion elements from the court by the working garment is an exception in our country and quickly disappeared. Abroad, however, it is quite frequent to find the field worker affecting a garment directly copying court fashion, as we see it in so many manuscripts of the period.

118.

Detail with sitting bathkeeper inset in grape-vine motif, f. 130, from the Bible of Wenceslas IV.

The development of the town and working garments in the 15th century proceeded at the same rate. The time-lag disappeared, the mutual relations between the creator of fashion (i. e. the royal court or town centre) and the recipient of new fashions (i. e. the working population) attained equilibrium. Both sides have now the same share in the development of fashion and both create fashion. Once it is the town detail, the so-called chemisette — inset piece of material — which influenced the development of the country chemise, then it is the country protecting apron which the town garment turns into a charming supplement of the Renaissance garment.

119.

WORKING DRESSES FROM THE MIDDLE OF THE 14th CENTURY
Detail with midwife, f. 41/c, drawn illustration of the manuscript Velislav Bible, before the middle of the 14th century. Cp. no. 13.

120. SIMPLE PATTERN, PRINTED MATERIAL

Detail of the garment of the Christ Child from the Madonna of Březnice, end of the 15th century.

Tempera painting on wood, 41×29.5 cm. Prague, National Gallery.

121.

WORKING DRESS FROM THE END OF THE 14th CENTURY

Detail with woman in labour, f. 110, from the first volume of the Bible of Wenceslas IV. Cp. no. 74.

122.

WORKING DRESSES OF THE MIDDLE OF THE 15th CENTURY
Detail from a birth scene, with midwife, whose dress was repainted later.

Master of Vyšší Brod, about 1350. (Cp. supplement V.)

191

123.

DETAIL WITH BED-SHEET
From the Death of the Virgin, f. 254. Liber Viaticus, before 1364.
Cp. no. 40.

The origin of the chemisette is controversial. As far as we can tell it is a purely Gothic detail, which originated as an inset piece of material in the undergarment which was visible under the open cloak.

The figure of Salome in the altarpiece at Zátoň (about 1430) presents the fundamental type of this new detail. Her garment of green colour is girded and has wide sleeves. The deep V of the neckline is picked out with pearls and reaches down to the waist; it is filled in with an inset made of red brocade with a high stand-up collar of the same material. It is the first inset we find portrayed not only in Bohemia but in the whole of Europe. It is interesting both for its early date and for its colour and cut. The insets of a later date are usually made of white materials, they form a kind of veil. The collar forming the end of the inset of Salome's garment is a reminiscence of the 14th century.

124.

DETAIL WITH SHEET,
f. 9, from the Krumlov Almanac of Religious Treatises. Cp. no. 4.

Insets were taken over about the middle of the century into paintings of almost all the saints and sometimes even of the Virgin. For example St. Margaret, small figure of a saint painted on the frame of the Vyšehrad Virgin of the type of the Virgin of St. Vitus Cathedral from about 1460, has a light coloured inset. It fits right up to the throat but does not form a collar. It is trimmed with lacing. The neckline is firmly stressed by the lacing. The lacing — a new Renaissance supplement of the garment — was taken over by folk costume together with the inset and was preserved in many countries. The lacing, chemisette, and bodice have since then become basic elements of the town and folk garment not only in Bohemia but even, for example, in Italy. Sometimes the lacing is functional, sometimes ornamental. To begin with it served the Renaissance division of garment and figure. However, it is an element emphasising both the functional aspect of the garment and the femininity of the figure.

193

125.

DETAIL WITH BED-SHEET AND BED COVER,
f. 9. From the Krumlov Almanac of Religious Treatises.

Cp. no. 4 and 124.

194

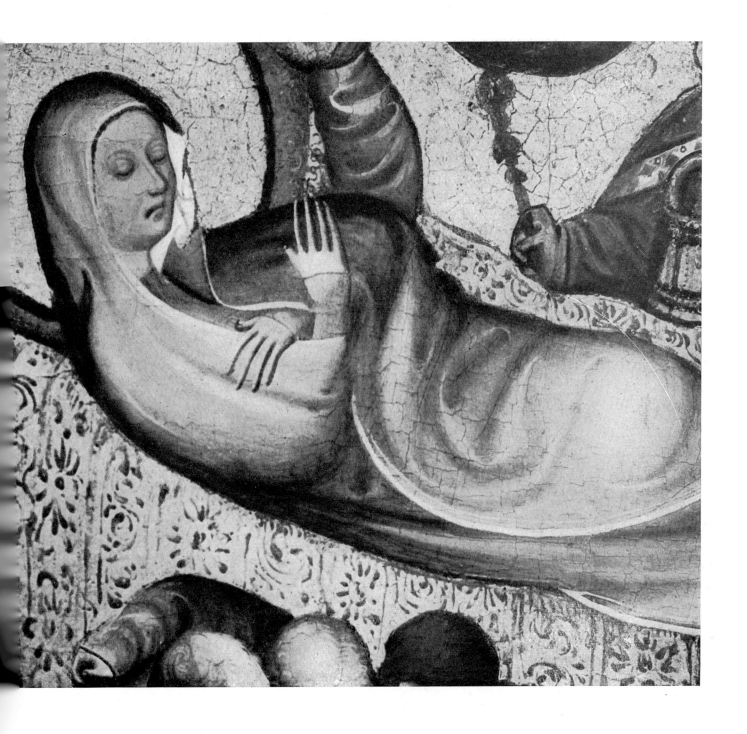

126.

Detail with sheet from the Death of the Virgin, Brno, about 1390.
Tempera painting on alder wood, 33.8 × 24 cm.

Probably made in some Moravian workshop.
Brno, Moravian Museum.

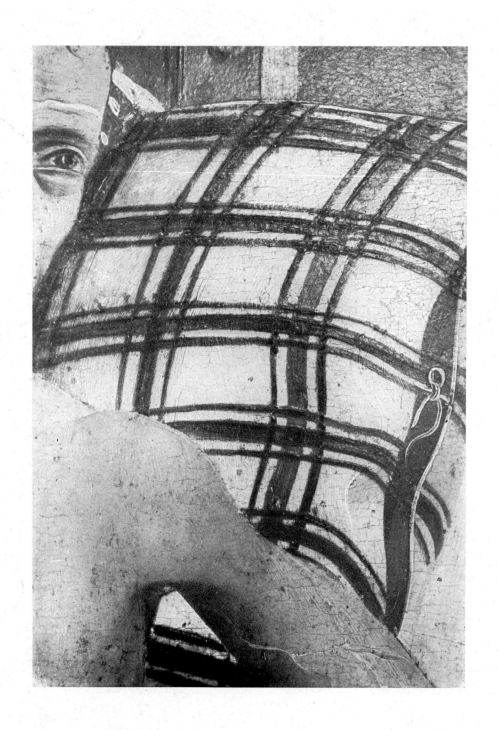

127.

Detail of cushion from the Beatified Anna Guardian, of 1482.

The painting forms part of the altar made at the order of Nicolas Puchner, Grandknight of the Order of the Knights of the Cross with a Red Star, who ordered it for the main altar of the originally Gothic church of St. Francis in the Old Town of Prague.

Prague, National Gallery.

Another interesting 15th century supplement to the dress is the cloak with collar; the cut of the cloak is traditional, but has as a new detail a small collar. This is the precursor of the Renaissance collar, and it originated in Southern Bohemia at the beginning of the 15th century.

Already the St. Margaret piece and after it all paintings of the saints and the Virgin from the 15th century show richly ornamented garments. In the period of Charles IV, when painters painted garments with the same pleasure as they do now, brocade was the main material. In the century under review the principal material was velvet combined either with brocade thread or cut.

The Assumption of Deštná (about 1450) shows for instance a draped undergarment with a beautiful pattern of cinquefoil. The 15th century painters showed more skill in painting textile patterns than the painters of the period of Charles IV. They use, however, the same method. The pomegranate pattern is spread over the surface very symmetrically, but the shadows are painted in later so skillfully that the person looking at the picture does not notice how much easier the painter made the work for himself.

128.

WORKING DRESSES WITH APRON FROM THE END
OF THE 14th CENTURY

Detail from The Message of the Amorites, f. 175, from the first volume of the Bible of Wenceslas IV.
Cp. no. 74.

129.

WORKING DRESSES WITH APRON FROM THE END
OF THE 14th CENTURY

Detail from Ruth Gleaning in the Field of Boaz, from the second volume of the Bible of Wenceslas IV.
Cp. no. 74.

130.

WORKING DRESSES FROM THE MIDDLE OF THE 15th CENTURY
SHOWING URBAN INFLUENCE
Detail from Ruth Gleaning in the Field of Boaz, drawing, f. 98b.

From the unfinished manuscript of the Old Testament, between 1430—1440.
Prague, National and University Library, sign. XVII A 34.

Materials with elaborate patterns, garments adorned with insets, hair curled at the ears and held with a net, berets, and crowns arranged in the shape of a beret, form the basis of town fashion of the 15th century.

It is a fashion all its own, its centre is not the royal court nor the Hussite camp, but it originated in the towns. In Bohemia it is for instance the fashion developed by Kutná Hora — famous even nowadays for the former richness of its silver mines, which enabled the town to build such buildings as the Church of St. Barbara.

131.

URBAN WORKING DRESSES FROM THE END OF THE 14th CENTURY
Detail from Women Weighing and Baking Bread, f. 128, from the first volume of the Bible of Wenceslas IV. Cp. 74.

131.

132. WORKING DRESS IN THE FIELD, UNDER THE INFLUENCE
OF TOWN FASHION

Breviary St. Georgii, Pars aestivalis, about 1400. Illumination to the Calendar, f. 4a.
Prague, National and University Library, sign. XIII C 1 a.

133.

TOWN DRESS WITH APRON FROM THE END
OF THE 14th CENTURY

Detail from the Samaritan Woman, f. 152, from the second volume of the Bible of Wenceslas IV.
Cp. no. 74.

134. PEASANT WORKING DRESS UNDER THE INFLUENCE OF THE
WENCESLAS FASHION

Olomouc Bible of 1417.

Detail from Ruth gleaning in the Field of Boaz, f. 114. Olomouc, Study Library.

135. Detail from the Judgement of King Solomon, f. 148. Olomouc Bible of 1417.
Olomouc, Study Library.

136.

CLOAKS WITH COLLAR

Detail with St. Ursula and St. Dorothy. From the frame of the Madonna of Vyšší Brod, after 1420.
Tempera painting on wood.

Originally intended perhaps for the Church of the Virgin Mary at Vyšší Brod, where it is still today.

XVI.

COATS WITH COLLAR
Detail with figures of St. Dorothy and St. Apollonia. Frame of the Madonna of St. Thomas, about 1420.

Tempera painting on lime wood.
The painting comes from the Church of St. Thomas in Brno.
Brno, Moravian Museum.

We must now return to the mural paintings and other representative works of art. We meet here again with elaborate materials, which give the substantial part of the ornamentation of the painting. Velvet and early Renaissance brocades produced in Florence spread all over Europe. In the mural paintings of the Smíšek Chapel in the Church of St. Barbara (1490) the principal motif is the pomegranate. It is greatly enlarged so as almost to obliterate the figure of the wearer. This pattern adorns the royal cloak as well as the Renaissance woman's garment, and veils the differently shaped woman's body also in a way different from that prescribed by the line from the end of the 14th century. The high-set bust corresponds to the high-placed waist, the deep neck-line shortens the bodice. Its depth is, however, covered by the heart-like cut inset, a light-coloured piece of material with golden hemming. The beret and inset have become the same fashion details as were formerly the veil and wimple. The garments of the ladies-in-waiting of the Queen of Sheba in the wall-paintings of Kutná Hora show how close the town garment is to the folk working garment, and how it differs only in trimming and material.

137.

CLOAKS WITH COLLAR
Visitation of the Virgin called the Ringhoffer Visitation. After 1430.

Tempera painting on wood, 100×70 cm.
Fragment of the altarpiece, probably connecting the Mary and the Passion cycle, attributed to the Master
of the Carrying of the Cross, of Vyšší Brod.

Prague, National Gallery.

XVII.

CLOAK WITH COLLAR

The Lanna Asumpta, about 1450.
Tempera painting on pine, 41.5 × 31.5 cm.
With original painted frame.

The painting was in the collection of the Prague collector V. Lanna, who bought it in 1883.
Prague, National Gallery.

The garments of the ladies-in-waiting — in patterned skirts with laced bodice — are made of precious and rare Italian velvet, but in principle they are identical with folk garments, as we shall see later. The skirt with bodice is pulled over the white chemise, the sleeves of which are reminiscent of the sleeves of national costumes. Only the beret making the skull fashionably long at the back is a temporary Renaissance supplement, which, however, did not last long, probably owing to its unnatural shape. But for this it may be said that the Renaissance town garment influenced the Sunday costume of peasant women.

138.

INSET WITH COLLAR

Salome with the head of St. John. Altarpiece from Zátoň, after 1430. Tempera painting on spruce, width 42 cm.

Right lower part of the three-partite altarpiece of altar with original framing.
The altar comes from the Church of St. John the Baptist at Zátoň in Southern Bohemia.
Prague, National Gallery.

XVIII. Detail from Salome, from the altar of Zátoň, cp. no. 138.

Only the queen and the ladies-in-waiting of the highest standing wear garments with long sleeves of the same material, reminiscent of ceremonial garments of former times. But the inset and crown, shaped in the form of a beret, give the Queen a Renaissance-like appearance as do also the wide and long skirts bordered with fur. The difference between the garment of the townswomen, who are presented here in the rôles of queens and ladies-in-waiting, and between the common market women of Kutná Hora, who have been portrayed in the so-called Graduale of Kutná Hora, is to be seen mainly in the length of the skirts. The beret is worn by all women. The inset and collar, a much liked detail, may be found on almost every garment of the period. However, the excessive length of skirt, which indicates high rank, is not found on town working garments. Even shorter is the skirt on the folk working garment, which now acquired its final form to remain as a legacy of the Renaissance preserved in many folk working costumes up to this day.

139. TEXTILE PATTERN, REPROD. VELVET

Detail of the dress from the Assumpta of Deštná, with pomegranate pattern (oldest example of this pattern in Bohemia), about 1450.

Tempera painting on pine wood, 114×111 cm. Prague, National Gallery.

140. Detail of St. Margaret, painting on the wooden frame of the Madonna of Vyšší Brod (St. Vitus type) about 1460. The painting comes perhaps from the Church of the Virgin Mary at Vyšší Brod. Now it is in the former monastery gallery.

140. LACING

The veils and the apron have been worn by working women since feudalism up till the 19th century. The length of the skirt varied according to what was practical. On their long journeys to town and at their field work women cannot, not even in their ripe old age, wear long skirts, which would only get dirty, and therefore they shorten them.

XIX.

LATE GOTHIC CUFFS AND RENAISSANCE LOW-CUT NECKLINE
Detail from the Beheading of St. Barbara, after 1540. Middle part of the three-partite altarpiece, coming probably from the monastery church of the Assumption of the Virgin Mary, at Osek, ascribed to Master I. W. and his assistant.

Tempera painting on wood, 141 × 111 cm.
Prague, National Gallery.

Nor could the towns woman continue to wear the Renaissance length of skirt. Therefore her garment is somewhat shortened but not so much as that of the peasant women. She, too, continued to wear a kind of wimple varying between a beret and a veil. In principle her garment stands midway between glorious town and peasant fashion. The town skirt with the bodice was provided with short sleeves, under which the white sleeves of the inner garment peep out. As a top protective garment the town working woman wore not only a short apron, but an apron up to the shoulders and protecting the garment both in front and at the back. The apron, this indispensable supplement of Bohemian working garments, became an adornment of town garments of the 16th century, the town fashion no longer imitated court fashion and was content with its own civic style.

141.

WORKING DRESS OF URBAN MARKET WOMEN
Detail from Life in the Mountains, after 1490.

From the Kutná Hora Graduale. The illuminations in the manuscript show everyday scenes of a miner's life depicted quite realistically. Vienna — State Library.

142.

URBAN WORKING DRESS WITH APRON

Detail from Life in the Mountains, after 1490.

From the Kutná Hora Graduale. Cp. no. 141.

143.

RENAISSANCE DRESS

Detail from the Sibylla of Tiburtin showing the Emperor Augustus the Madonna and prophesying him the coming of the Saviour. East wall of the Smíšek Chapel in the Church of St. Barbara, Kutná Hora, about 1490. Kutná Hora, originally a small mining settlement, grew to be a great and important mining town under Wenceslas II (1278—1305). It continued to grow in wealth and steadily developed until the Renaissance. It built a great church dedicated to St. Barbara, the patron saint of miners. Master Smíšek of Vrchoviště was one of the patricians of Kutná Hora who did much for the town, and one of the chapels in the Church of St. Barbara bears his name.

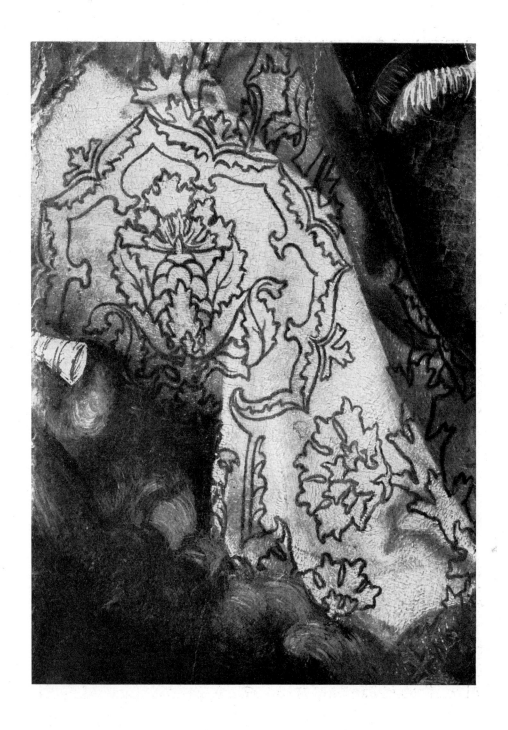

144.

SAMPLE OF A RENAISSANCE TEXTILE PATTERN WITH POMEGRANATE
Detail from the Coronation of the Virgin from the altar of Osek, about 1520.

Painting on lime wood, 150.5 × 100.5 cm.
Centre of the three-partite altarpiece.
Prague, National Gallery.

145.

SAMPLE OF A LARGE RENAISSANCE TEXTILE PATTERN
WITH POMEGRANATE

Detail from the Annunciation, end of the 15th century.
Rakovník, Town Museum.

146. RENAISSANCE BERET

Detail of the wall painting of the Crucifixion. Kutná Hora, Church of St. Barbara, Smíšek Chapel, cp. no. 143.

147. Renaissance chasuble of cut velvet (original) from Budyň nad Ohří.
Prague, National Museum.

148. LOW-CUT NECKLINE, HAIRDRESS AND ARRANGEMENT O.F THE BERET

Mary Magdalene from Malý Bor near Horažďovice, about 1520. Detail of a wooden plastic.
České Budějovice, Municipal Museum.

147.

148.

Contrary to the town garment, which has been developing with many variations since the 15th century, the peasant working garment remained a Renaissance garment.

At the beginning of our study we asked why the word *mode* for fashion arose just in the 15th century. We are now in a position to answer that question, for, as we have shown, it was in that century that the fashion of the court and of the townspeople began to diverge from that of the country people, and entered upon a development of its own, while in the country no real development took place. Thus the contrast between mobile court and town and firmly rooted countryside drew attention to the development and changes in wearing apparel as such, and the new conception thus born demanded verbal expression, and with that the old Latin word came to denote that which ever changes in the appearance of man. It is this change at its most interesting time which is so very well shown in the Bohemiam manuscripts and paintings and from whose wellnigh inexhaustible wealth I have here given some examples.

149. RENAISSANCE ARRANGEMENT OF THE HEAD-DRESS
Detail of the Tiburtine Sibylla.

Kutná Hora, Church of St. Barbara, Smíšek Chapel.
Cp. nos. 143.

150. CEREMONIAL RENAISSANCE DRESS
Detail from the Queen of Sheba crossing the Water, about 1490.

Cp. no. 151, 153.

151. RENAISSANCE ARRANGEMENT OF THE HEAD-DRESS
Detail from the Queen of Sheba, about 1490.

Kutná Hora, Church of St. Barbara, Smíšek Chapel.
Cp. nos. 150, 153.

152. RENAISSANCE BERET AND LOW-CUT NECKLINE
Detail from Trajan's Justice, about 1490.

Kutná Hora, Church of St. Barbara, Smíšek Chapel.
Cp. no. 143.

153. URBAN RENAISSANCE DRESSES
Detail of the mural painting of the Queen of Sheba crossing the Water, about 1490.

Kutná Hora, Church of St. Barbara, Smíšek Chapel.
Cp. nos. 143, 150, 151.

149.

150.

151.

152.

153.

LITERATURE CONSULTED

It was in the 16th century that books on costume began to make their appearance. Dress was regarded as a distinguishing mark of one's station in society. This type of costume literature dealt primarily with the dress of kings and clergy, soldiers and commoners. The most natural division of garments into men's and women's garments was first introduced in literature on costume by the German designer Amman, whose drawings reveal his realistic approach to the world round him. During the 17th century, in the Baroque period, costume literature grew to such an extent that it must be regarded as a literary genre of its own. At the same time it began to change from specialised costume literature into *collections of fashion engravings*. These engravings are devoted to the women's garments of the time, or in short to fashion proper.

The final stage of this development occurred in the 18th century, when the place of the specialised literature on costume was taken by fashion journals serving everyday needs. The 18th century was a period of highly developed fashion, and, in France especially, with regard to men's dress. Hence the French fashion engravings acquired commercial importance as they could be used easily for providing other countries with French designs, whereas in the past all knowledge of French fashion outside France had had to be obtained from travellers. The new approach of the French fashion engravings shows itself also in the inclusion of engravings displaying the garments worn by the various trades; thus they bear witness to a prerevolutionary interest in the broad masses.

Instead of the elegant engravings of the 18th century we have in the 19th century much more specialised costume literature. We have dictionaries dealing with special aspects of the subject such as the dresses worn in the various parts of the country. The costume literature of the 19th century falls into three distinct periods, roughly corresponding to the periods of Enlightenment, Romanticism and Positivism. At the beginning of the century we still have the interest in the antique dress, which towards the end of the 18th century served as a model for contemporary fashion.

The second period, that corresponding to romanticism in literature, abandoned the antique fashion in favour of national and medieval costume. Artists and historical archeologists began to take an interest in the question of medieval costume, which had been neglected for so long. This first wave of interest in the medieval garment resulted in a long series of works of which we shall mention only the three most important ones: F. Hegi, *Das Costume des Mittelalters* (1807); Pinelli et C. Hullmandel, *Roman Costumes* (1820); C. Bonnard et P. Mercuri, *Costumi de'secoli XIIIe, XIVe, XVe* (1828). Besides these, however, we have also books which pay more specific attention to the artistic aspect of costume. These books are almost all written by Italian and Swiss scholars, whose interest in the artistic aspect of costume then later developed into an interest in costume as such, and gave rise to books of a more instructive kind. From among these books we may specially mention the following ones: H. Wagner, *Trachtenbuch des Mittel-Alters* (1830-34); J. H. v. Hefner-Alteneck, *Trachten des christlichen Mittelalters* (1840-54); J. Falke, *Zur Costumgeschichte des Mittel-Alters* (1861); P. Lacroix et F. Séré, *Le Moyen Age et la Renaissance* (1848-51); J. Labarte, *Histoire des arts industriels au Moyen-Age* (1864-66); K. Köhler und E. v. Sichard, *Praktische Kostümskunde in 600 Bildern und Schnitten* (Munich, 1926) and from the dictionary literature, Victor Gay, *Glossaire archéologique du moyen-âge et de la renaissance* (Paris, 1887-1928); C. Enlart, *Manuel d'archéologie française*, vol. III: *Le costume* (1916). These books succeeded in establishing a systematic treatment of the subject which is still valid today. By the beginning of the 19th century so much had been written about costume that bibliographies of fashion literature made their appearance.

Books dealing exclusively with women's costume in the Middle Ages are much rarer than books belonging to the category of general literature on costume. This in itself is only natural, and the beginning of these books was modest indeed. Thus one of the earliest ones, Edmond le Chevallier-Chevignard, *Costumes historiques de femmes du XIVe au XVIIIe* (Paris, 1889), was, for instance, a mere reprint of excerpts from Bonnard et Mercuri, a book mentioned above. Sometimes such books were also written to serve as a guide to producers of dramas and plays dealing with the Middle Ages as, for instance, Thomas Hailes Lacy, *Female Costumes, Historical, National and Dramatic* (London, 1865). Hardly any books dealing with women's costume appeared before the 20th century; of these we may mention especially Theodore Child, *Wimples and Crisping Pin Studies in the Coiffure* (New York, 1895); E. Roehl, *Die Tracht der schlesischen Fürstinnen des 13. und 14. Jahrhunderts* (Breslau, 1895). It is interesting to note that the British writers are interested in the garments of the peasant women of the 16th and 17th centuries, that the Italian writers concentrate on the Renaissance period, and that it is left to the French to deal with this question in all centuries; there is one exception to this general rule, *viz.* E. R. Goddard, *Women's Costume in French Texts of the XIth and XIIth Centuries*, and that book was published not in London but in — Paris (1927).

The Bohemian costume from the period of the Luxembourgs has been described many times (Zíbrt, Winter, Tomek) and evaluated from the cultural-historical point of view. Thus for instance we find it mentioned in connection with studies of tablets (Chytil), of manuscripts (Matějček) or materials and garments found for example in the royal vault at St. Vitus' Cathedral (Gollerová-Plachá, Lejsková). It has been treated in various connections but not directly related to the question of fashion.

BIBLIOGRAPHIES

René Colas: Bibliographie générale du Costume et de la Mode. Paris 1933. I—II.

I. Monro and D. E. Cook: Costume Index. New York 1937.

M. Davenport: The Book of Costume. New York 1948. I—II. (With a detailed bibliography of fashion.)

BOOKS ON FASHION AND TEXTILES QUOTED IN THE TEXT

J. Falke: Zur Costümgeschichte der Culturvölker. Stuttgart 1881.

Č. Zíbrt: Dějiny kroje v zemích českých od dob nejstarších až po války husitské. (History of costumes in the Bohemian lands from the oldest times to the Hussite Wars.) Praha 1892.

Z. Winter: Dějiny kroje v zemích českých od počátku století 15. až po dobu bělohorské bitvy. (History of costumes in the Bohemian lands from the beginning of the 15th century to the time of the Battle on the White Mountain.) Praha 1893.

O. v. Falke: Kunstgeschichte der Seidenweberei. Berlin 1913.

H. Floerke: Die Moden der italienischen Renaissance. München 1917.

E. v. Sichart: Praktische Kostümkunde. München 1926.

M. Lejsková: Dvojí šat královen z hrobky českých králů v chrámu sv. Víta. (Two costumes of queens from the tomb of the Bohemian kings in the St. Vitus Cathedral.) Památky archeologické. Praha 1931, pp. 5—9.

J. Vydra: Nauka o kroji. (Nově přepracováno podle knihy R. Tyršové.) Study of costumes — newly revised after the book of R. Tyršová. Praha 1931.

J. Wagenknecht: Krejčí v Praze od založení města až po dnešní doby. (Tayloring in Prague from the foundation of the town till the present day.) Praha 1932—1933. I—II.

J. Gollerová-Plachá: Látky z pražské královské hrobky. (Textiles from the royal tombs in Prague.) Praha 1934.

A. L. Gutmann: Flanderisches Tuch in Kunst und Mode. Basel 1937.

L. G. Deruisseau: Die Entwicklung der Moden während der italienischen Renaissance. Basel 1937.

W. Steinmann: Ständetrachten im Mittelalter. Basel 1938.

W. Steinmann: Zwangstrachten im Mittelalter. Basel 1938.

L. Hurníková: Gothic Wowen Textiles in Bohemia. Unpublished doctor's thesis.

Jul. Schlosser: Die Bilderhandschriften König Wenzels IV. Jahrbuch d. W. Kg. XIV (1893).

WORKS CONSULTED FOR HISTORICAL DATA

J. Neuwirth: Das Braunschweiger Skizzenbuch eines mittelalterlichen Malers. 1897.

F. J. Lehner: Česká škola malířská XI. věku. (The Bohemian school of painters of the XIth century.) Praha 1902.

A. Matějček: Pasionál abatyše Kunhuty. (The Passion-Book of the Abbess Kunhuta.) Praha 1922.

A. Matějček: Dějepis umění. (History of Art.) Part II. Praha 1924.

A. Matějček: Velislavova bible. (The Velislav Bible.) Praha 1926.

A. Friedl: Iluminace Gumpoldovy legendy o sv. Václavu ve Wolfenbüttelu. (The Illumination of Gumpold's legend of St. Wencelslas in Wolfenbüttel.) Praha 1926.

J. Květ: Italské vlivy na pozdně románskou knižní malbu v Čechách. (Italian influences on Late Romanesque illumination in Bohemia.) Praha 1927.

K. Chytil: Umění české na počátku 15. století. (Bohemian art at the beginning of the 15th century.) Part II, Journal, Umění (The Arts), Praha 1929.

V. Birnbaum, J. Cibulka, A. Matějček, J. Pečírka, V. V. Štech: Dějepis výtvarného umění v Čechách. (History of painting and sculpture in Bohemia.) Part I, Praha 1931.

A. Goldschmidt: Die Bronzetüren von Nowgorod und Gnesen. Marburg a. L. 1932.
Jihočeská gotika ve sbírkách městského musea v Českých Budějovicích. (South Bohemian Gothic in the collections of the Municipal Museum in České Budějovice.) Praha 1936.

K. Stloukal: Královny, kněžny a velké ženy české. (Queens, princesses and great women of Bohemia.) Praha 1940.

K. Šourek: Miniatury české bible zvané Boskovské z let 1420—1430 v studijní knihovně v Olomouci. (Miniatures of the Czech so-called Boskov Bible of the years 1420—1430 in the study library in Olomouc.) Praha 1944.

K. Šourek: Miniatury dvoudílné české bible zvané Olomoucké z roku 1417 ve studijní knihovně v Olomouci. (Miniatures in the Czech so-called Olomouc Bible in two volumes of 1417 in the study library in Olomouc.) Praha 1944.

K. Šourek: Gotická plastika XIV. století v domě Sv. Víta v Praze. (Gothic plastic of the XIVth century in the St Vitus Cathedral in Prague.) Praha 1944.

K. Šourek: Nástěnné a deskové malířství na Karlštejně. (Mural and tablet painting of the castle Karlštejn.) Unpublished.

D. Menclová: Hrad Karlštejn. (Castle Karlštejn.) Praha 1946.

V. Chaloupecký, J. Květ and *V. Mencl:* Praha románská (Romanesque Prague.) Praha 1948.

A. Kutal, D. Líbal, A. Matějček: České umění gotické (Bohemian Gothic art.) Praha 1949.
Česká malba gotická. Deskové malířství 1350—1450. (Bohemian Gothic painting. Tablet paintings 1350—1450.) Praha 1950.

J. Pešina: Česká malba pozdní gotiky a renesance. (Bohemian painting of the Late Gothic and of the Renaissance.) Praha 1950.

RESUME

LA MODE ET LE COSTUME

Le mot »mode« n'apparaît dans la littérature française qui est pour notre sujet la plus importante qu'au courant du XVIIe siècle. Encore au XVIe siècle, où la forme du vêtement se modifie souvent, les ouvrages littéraires français se contentent du mot »costume«. L'essor rapide de la culture vestimentaire en France durant le XVIIe siècle a pour conséquence l'emploi plus large du mot »mode« qui est dès lors utilisé aussi dans d'autres secteurs de la vie et passe dans la littérature et le langage d'autres pays. Le mot »costume« reste à cette époque réservé à certains groupes sociaux et ethnographiques comme par exemple le costume de paysan ou le costume oriental. A partir du XVIIIe siècle on emploie le mot »mode« non seulement pour la mode contemporaine, mais aussi dans les traités historiques s'occupant de l'évolution des costumes (Histoire des modes françaises).

L'histoire scientifique et culturelle du développement du vêtement qui débute au début du XIXe siècle emploie presque uniquement le mot »costume«, mais plus tard (Boehn) elle se sert de l'expression »mode« dans toutes les branches de l'histoire. Si dans la littérature anglaise et américaine moderne nous trouvons seulement le mot »costume«, c'est moins par conservativisme que pour une raison linguistique. Les Anglais ont traduit le mot mode en »fashion«, qui pourtant est loin de donner toute la signification que les Français attachent à ce mot.

Dans notre publication le mot »mode« est utilisé pour désigner la période de l'histoire dont elle traite bien qu'il fût peu usité à cette époque. Par la »mode« il faut en effet entendre les évolutions du costume d'une époque, l'élément révélateur et dynamique de l'histoire du costume.

Littérature traitant l'histoire de la mode

Dès le XVIe siècle apparaissent en Italie et en France des traités scientifiques sur l'habillement dans différents pays qui sont en quelque sorte un complément de la littérature ethnographique de l'époque. Le XVIIe siècle et encore plus le XVIIIe sont caractérisés par des recueils de gravures de costumes contemporains qui se transforment peu à peu en une sorte de catalogues, précurseurs des journaux de modes actuels. Toutefois ce qui est important pour cet ouvrage, c'est la littérature scientifique et historique du romantisme qui a découvert le costume du moyen âge et qui est restée jusqu'à nos jours la base de nos connaissances dans ce secteur. Le point de vue de cette publication en diffère par le fait qu'elle regarde la mode comme un reflet direct des beaux-arts de l'époque contemporaine d'autant plus que les peintures et les sculptures en sont la source principale.

La littérature qui traite la mode et le costume a toujours été influencée par la classe dirigeante de l'époque. Dans le grand nombre d'ouvrages qui s'occupent de ce sujet, on n'en trouvera aucun se consacrant à la description du costume des classes ouvrières. La littérature la plus ancienne nous renseigne sur la mode de la cour et du clergé et sur les costumes militaires. Plus tard elle commence à s'occuper aussi de la mode féminine et des costumes des différents états et corps de métier. Au XVIIIe siècle elle va même jusqu'à s'intéresser aussi au »costume« des classes ouvrières, mais il ne s'agit pas là de leur vêtement de travail.

Progression méthodique de notre ouvrage

Notre publication poursuit le but de reconstituer le costume féminin en Bohême entre l'année 1000 et l'année 1500 d'après miniatures, panneaux, peintures murales et sculptures. Jusqu'à présent, ce sujet a été étudié généralement du point de vue historiquement culturel. Nous l'abordons en appliquant uniquement les méthodes de l'histoire de l'art; nous regardons le costume non en tant qu'élément isolé, mais comme l'expression des moyens de fabrication et des conditions matérielles dont nous cherchons le reflet dans la coupe des vêtements et surtout dans le tissu dont ils sont confectionnés.

Dans la première période dont s'occupe notre publication, la confection des vêtements a adopté un genre visiblement ornemental et la couture est cachée par des ourlets qui décomposent le costume plastiquement en plusieurs éléments isolés comme le fait l'architecture de l'époque. Le costume de l'époque romane est la continuation directe de la robe antique dont les éléments fondamentaux sont contenus encore de nos jours dans les vêtements liturgiques catholiques (chasuble, dalmatique etc.). Les détails ont subi l'influence de Byzance qui était aussi le fournisseur principal des tissus destinés aux classes riches. Les sources principales concernant cette époque nous apprennent que le costume des classes pauvres avait la même coupe que celui des classes dirigeantes et n'en différait que par la qualité inférieure des tissus, le nombre plus restreint de jupes et le manque de bordures. Il est caractéristique que le costume des femmes ne se distingue presque pas de celui des hommes.

L'exploitation rurale à la fin du régime de l'esclavage ne permet pas encore la division du travail et par suite le costume, confectionné à la maison, n'a à sa disposition, même en ce qui concerne les tissus importés, que des étoffes d'une certaine largeur qui se coupent transversalement c'est-à-dire de la façon la plus simple. Ce type de vêtement se retrouve en principe dans le costume actuel des montagnards en Slovaquie. La pièce fondamentale en est la chemise d'homme, confectionnée d'une bande de tissu dans laquelle on a découpé une ouverture pour la tête et qui a été complétée de manches droites.

Dans la période qui suit, c'est-à-dire celle du régime féodal, la différenciation sociale commence à se faire remarquer dans le costume, car celui des classes pauvres obligées de travailler ne se compose tout d'abord que d'un vêtement de base porté par les classes dirigeantes comme vêtement de dessous. Chez les femmes il s'agit toujours d'une sorte de chemise devenue collante, à manches longues et descendant jusqu'aux chevilles. Le vêtement des hommes commence à se distinguer de celui des femmes tout en l'influençant, toutefois, par ses ornements et divers détails. Par ailleurs le costume des religieuses se distingue de celui des autres femmes et le vêtement de jeunes filles de celui des femmes mariées. Le costume de dame des classes dirigeantes présente une grande variété de détails. C'est également à partir de cette époque que la coiffure devient partie intégrante du costume. A la suite de la division du travail qui donne naissance aux divers corps de métier, les vêtements commencent à être confectionnés sur mesure par des ouvriers qualifiés qui s'efforcent de faire ressortir les lignes du corps féminin. C'est l'origine de la robe collante gothique qui devint le point de départ du costume féminin des siècles suivants .

L'influence de la mode française qui ressort des documents littéraires tchèques de la première moitié du XIVe siècle et qui fit provisoirement place à celle de Byzance dans la seconde moitié de ce siècle, époque du règne de Charles IV, s'est encore accentuée sous le règne de Venceslas IV. C'est la période d'or de la mode tchèque où le costume de la femme tchèque, surtout celui de la cour, a pleinement réalisé l'idéal de l'époque. Dans la mode se reflète aussi le formalisme accentué de la période du »beau style« qui caractérise l'art gothique tchèque vers l'année 1400. Le costume donne une nouvelle ligne au corps féminin, la taille descend sur les hanches accentuant ainsi sa fonction érotique et un décolleté plus osé découvre les épaules. Ainsi fut créée la ligne la plus expressive jusqu'alors connue du vêtement féminin, ligne que l'on ne retrouvera plus même dans le courant de plusieurs siècles suivants.

Un fait très important pour l'évolution ultérieure du costume est la transformation de la robe jusqu'alors en une pièce en corsage et jupe. Cette transformation continue ensuite en séparant du corsage la gorgerette destinée à recouvrir partiellement le décolleté. En même temps le corsage devient plus petit et se transforme en corset.

Il suffit alors de raccourcir la jupe et d'ajouter le tablier pour obtenir le costume de paysan qui s'est dès lors stabilisé et a donné naissance au costume de fête de la femme paysanne. L'importance de cet ouvrage, qui s'arrête à l'année 1500, ressort donc du fait que vers cette date naquit le vêtement de travail — le costume de fête populaire.

Ce vêtement, toutefois, ne se transforme que très lentement, car grâce à sa forme extrêmement pratique, il convenait au travail; il ne fut définitivement remplacé que récemment par la mode actuelle très en vogue et adoptée universellement par toutes les femmes de ce pays, les pantalons d'homme.

CATALOGUE

Tableau n° 1. VÊTEMENT DE L'EMPEREUR VERS L'AN 1000

Détail du frontispice

Légende de St Venceslas (écrite par Gumpold, évêque de Mentoue, à la demande de l'empereur Otta II). Copie enluminée, préparée sur l'ordre de la princesse Emma, épouse de Boleslav II, entre 1000 et 1006.

Manuscrit de l'école de Fulda.

Ancienne bibliothèque de Wolfenbüttel.

Tableau n° 2. ETOFFE DE SOIE AVEC APPLICATIONS

Elle provient du couvercle du tombeau de St Venceslas, Ière moitié du XIIe siècle.

Première mentionnée dans l'inventaire de la cathédrale de St Guy, Prague, 1387.

Prague, musée de la capitale.

Tableau n° 3. MODELE DE TISSU

Détail de l'initiale I (prophète Aggeus et frère Godefridus), sur le folio 171 de la Bible de St François, fin du XIIIe siècle. Le manuscrit provient du monastère des franciscains de la Vielle Ville, qui fut fondé en 1234, en même temps que le couvent des clarisses; ce fut la première construction gothique à Prague. Bibliothèque du Musée national, cote XII B 13.

Tableau n° 4. MODELE DE TISSU

Détail d'une miniature du folio 346 du manuscrit

»Livret sur la mort d'un jeune homme fougueux«, Ier quart du XVe siècle.

Recueil des traités religieux dits de Krumlov.

Prague, Bibliothèque du Musée national, III B 10.

Tableau n° 5. Légende de St Adalbert.

Bas-relief en bronze de l'époque romane sur la porte de la cathédrale du Hnězdno polonais.

Vers 1150.

Remarquable monument de l'art roman du fondage en Europe centrale. Il atteste de l'existence de relations fort anciennes entre la Pologne et Prague.

Détail de la scène »La naissance de St Adalbert«.

Tableau n° 6. VÊTEMENT DE TRAVAIL DE L'EPOQUE ROMANE

L'Evangile de la couronne.

Détail du tableau, au folio 41, avec la scène »Les trois reniements de Pierre«.

Tableau n° 7. COSTUME DE SOCIETE DE L'EPOQUE ROMANE

Evangile de la couronne, dit Codex de Vyšehrad.

Le Codex date sans aucun doute du couronnement du roi de Bohême Vratislav, en 1085.

Le manuscrit, d'une exceptionnelle richesse au point de vue iconographique, est l'oeuvre d'un atelier du pays, atelier duquel sont encore sortis plusieurs autres livres d'une incomparable richesse d'illustration.

Il a anciennement appartenu à l'église St Guy, puis à l'église de Vyšehrad à Prague.

Prague, Bibliothèque nationale et universitaire, XIV A 13.

Détail du tableau sur le folio 19b, avec la scène »Le sacrifice au temple«.

Tableau n° 8. HABIT DE RELIGIEUSE

Détail de l'initiale »P«.

Antiphonaire de Sedlec. Première moitié du XIIIe siècle.

Le manuscrit a été préparé pour un certain couvent de Bohême.

Prague, Bibliothèque nationale et universitaire, XIII A 6.

Tableau n° 9. HABIT DE RELIGIEUSES

Passionnaire de l'abbesse Kunhuta. Le manuscrit a été commandé vers 1320 par l'abbesse Kunhuta, supérieure du couvent de St Georges au Hradčany de Prague. Kunhuta était la fille de Přemysl Otakar II, roi de Bohême. Sur le frontispice, elle est représentée avec le copiste du Passionnaire, Kolda, son enlumineur Beneš et des religieuses.

Détail du folio 1b.

Prague, Bibliothèque nationale et universitaire, cote XIV A 17.

Tableau n° 10. ROBE DE CELIBATAIRE VERS 1320

Détail d'une miniature de la scène »Ecclesia militans«, au folio 22b. Passionnaire de l'abbesse Kunhuta, Voir n° 9.

Tableau n° 11. ROBE DE FEMME MARIEE, VERS 1320

Détail d'une miniature de la scène »Ecclesia militans«, au folio 22b. Passionnaire de l'abbesse Kunhuta, Voir n° 9.

Tableau n° 12. MANTEAU MODERNE, AVEC BANDE AUTOUR DU COL, VERS 1320

Détail d'une miniature avec scènes de la parabole sur le vaillant chevalier, folio 3b.

Pour autres renseignements, voir n° 9, Passionnaire de l'abbesse Kunhuta.

Tableau n° 13. VETEMENT DE TRAVAIL DE JEUNE FEMME

Détail d'une illustration au folio 126a.

Bible de Velislav.

Velislav (vraisemblablement chancelier de l'empereur Charles IV) qui a fait faire cette bible avant le milieu du XIVe siècle est représenté à la fin du livre, agenouillé devant Sainte Catherine. Au manuscrit se trouve annexé le cycle sur l'Antéchrist, puis des fragments du cycle sur la semaine sainte et les actes apostoliques, le cycle de l'Apocalypse et la légende de St Venceslas. La bible contient 747 illustrations dessinées à la plume.

Prague, Bibliothèque nationale et universitaire, cote Lob. 412.

Tableau n° 14. VETEMENT DE TRAVAIL

Détail d'une illustration. Bible de Velislav.

Tableau n° 15. ROBES DE SOCIETE DE JEUNES DAMES

Détail d'une illustration. Bible de Velislav.

Tableau n° 16. MANIERE MODERNE DE DRAPER LE MANTEAU; GESTES ET ACCESSOIRES SEYANT AUX DAMES AGEES AU MILIEU DU XIVe SIECLE

Détail d'une illustration. Bible de Velislav.

Tableau nº 23. DEUX GENRES DE DESSINS FONDAMENTAUX GOTHIQUES

Détail du vêtement d'un apôtre.
L'Ascension, vers 1350.
Maître de Vyšší Brod.
Peinture en détrempe sur bois, H. 95 cm, L. 85,5 cm.

Tableau nº 24. DESSIN D'ETOFFE GOTHIQUE

Détail du vêtement du roi.
Adoration des mages, vers 1350.
Maître de Vyšší Brod.
Peinture en détrempe sur bois, H. 95 cm, L. 85,5 cm.

Annexe IV.

Maître de Vyšší Brod.
Adoration des mages.

Tableau nº 25. IMITATION LIBRE EN PEINTURE D'UN DESSIN GOTHIQUE

Détail du coussin de la Madone.
La Nativité.
Maître de Vyšší Brod.
Peinture en détrempe sur bois, H. 95 cm, L. 85,5 cm.

Annexe V.

Maître de Vyšší Brod.
La Nativité.

Tableau nº 26. Détail du manteau de Charles IV. Modèle de textile contemporain. Voir Annexe VI.

Annexe VI.

Tableau votif de Jan Očko de Vlašim, après 1370.
Peinture en détrempe sur bois, H. 181 cm, L. 96 cm.
Le tableau a été commandé par l'archevêque Jan Očko, secrétaire de l'empereur Charles IV, pour la nouvelle chapelle du château archiépiscopal de Roudnice. Il représente Charles IV et Venceslas IV agenouillés devant la Madone avec St Venceslas et St Sigismond dans la partie supérieure. Dans la partie inférieure s'agenouille le donateur du tableau; à gauche St Procope, St Adalbert, à droite St Guy et Ste Ludmila.
Détail de la partie supérieure du tableau.
Reproduction montrant son état avant sa restauration.
Prague, Galerie nationale.

Tableaux nᵒˢ:

27. Détail du manteau de Jan Očko. Voir annexe VI.
28. Détail du manteau de St Adalbert. Voir annexe VI.
29. Détail du manteau de St Adalbert. Voir annexe VI.
30. Détail du manteau de Jan Očko. Voir annexe VI.
Suprême élégance de la ligne gothique tchèque à la fin du XIVe siècle. Presque toutes les oeuvres d'art de ce style qui ont été conservées se trouvent sur le territoire du sud de la Bohême et elles se rattachent pour la plupart à la petite ville de Třeboň. Třeboň a donné son nom au plus grand peintre du moyen-âge tchèque, au »Maître de Třeboň« et son nom est également lié aux fameuses »belles madones« tchèques, dont l'une des plus célèbres est appelée »La Madone de Třeboň«.

Annexe VII.

Maître du retable de Třeboň, vers 1380.

Ste Catherine, Ste Madeleine, Ste Marguerite. Côté extérieur du panneau »Le Christ au jardin des Oliviers«. Peinture en détrempe sur bois de tilleul, H. 132 cm, L. 92 cm. Vraisemblablement partie de l'autel de l'époque dans l'église St Gilles de Třeboň.

Prague, Galerie nationale.

Tableau n° 31. MANTEAU ET VOILE DE JEUNES FEMMES

Détail d'une Madone.

Adoration de l'Enfant Jésus à Hluboká. Peinture en détrempe sur bois, H. 125 cm, L. 95 cm.

Ecole du Maître de Třeboň, avant 1400.

Le château de Hluboká.

Tableau n° 32. MANTEAUX ET CEINTURES DE FEMMES AGEES

Le Crucifiement, église de Ste Barbe, avant 1400.

Peinture en détrempe sur bois de pin. H. 125 cm, L. 95 cm.

Prague, Galerie nationale.

Tableau n° 33. MANTEAU AVEC COL

Détail avec Ste Marguerite.

Cadre peint du tableau de la Madone Aracoeli, largeur du cadre 11 cm, bois.

Ecole du Maître de Třeboň, vers 1400.

Prague, Galerie nationale.

Tableau n° 34. MANTEAU TRADITIONNEL

Détail avec Ste Apolena.

Cadre peint du tableau de la Madone Aracoeli. Pour autres renseignements, voir n° 33.

Ecole du Maître de Třeboň, vers 1400.

Tableau n° 35. Madone de Třeboň, vers 1390.

Statuette de pierre, hauteur 124 cm. Polychromie d'une époque ultérieure.

Třeboň, église de St Gilles.

Tableau n° 36. DETAIL D'UNE AGRAFE DU VETEMENT DE S^T VENCESLAS

Triptyque avec la Madone, St Venceslas et St Palmacius.

Tomasso da Modena, Ecole italienne, 1357—67.

Peinture en détrempe sur bois.

Karlštejn, chapelle de la Sainte Croix.

Tableau n° 37. COIFFURE EN FORME DE GUIMPE

Détail de la scène »Le Crucifiement«, d'un maître inconnu de l'entourage de l'école de peinture de la cour de Prague; vers 1365.

Peinture murale du fronton de l'autel de la chapelle Ste Catherine à Karlštejn.

Annexe VIII.

Madone de Rome, vers 1360.

Peinture en détrempe sur bois de hêtre, H. 22 cm, L. 16,5 cm.

Prague, Galerie nationale.

Tableau n° 38. MANTEAU TRADITIONNEL AVEC AGRAFE ET LA NOUVELLE MANIERE DE LE PORTER VERS LE MILIEU DU XIVE SIECLE

Détail d'une initiale avec la Madone.

Orationale d'Arnošt de Pardubice, vers 1360.

Le manuscrit fut commandé par le premier archevêque de Prague, Arnošt de Pardubice, l'un des participants du mouvement tchèque et européen de la Réforme.

Prague, bibliothèque du Musée national, cote XIII C 12.

Tableau n° 39. LIGNE TYPIQUE DU VETEMENT GOTHIQUE

Détail avec Marie.

Tableau recouvrant le folio 55b, avec la scène de l'Annonciation. Laus Mariae de Konrad de Haimburk, manuscrit enluminé intitulé »Mariale«. Vers 1364.

Prague, bibliothèque du Musée national, cote XVI D 13.

Tableau n° 40. BANDEAU, VOILE ET COIFFURE

Détail de l'initiale »O«, avec l'Adoration des rois. F. 97. Liber viaticus, 1364.

Le manuscrit fut commandé par l'évêque de Litomyšl, Jan de Středa, comme bréviaire de voyage.

Prague, bibliothèque du Musée national, XIII A 12.

Annexe IX.

DIADEME AVEC COURONNE ET VOILE ET MANTEAU AVEC CAPUCHON

Madone de Veveří. Vers 1350.

Peinture en détrempe sur bois de pin. H. 79 cm, L. 63 cm.

Provient de la chapelle funéraire de l'Assomption qui se trouve près du château de Veveří en Moravie.

Prague, Galerie nationale.

Tableau n° 41. GUIMPE FORMEE D'UN VOILE

Détail de la scène du Sacrifice au temple sur le folio 209.

Liber viaticus 1364. Voir tableau 40.

Prague, Bibliothèque du Musée national.

Tableau n° 42. VOILE AVEC BORDURE NOIRE

Détail de Marie-Madeleine du »Crucifiement«.

Peinture en détrempe sur bois. H. 95 cm, L. 85,5 cm.

Maître de Vyšší Brod. Vers 1350.

Voir II.

Prague, Galerie nationale.

Annexe X.

MANTEAUX PASSES PAR-DESSUS LA TETE

Le Crucifiement.

Maître de Vyšší Brod, vers 1350. Voir annexe II.

Tableau n° 43. COIFFURE DE FEMME AGEE. VOILE, DIADEME ET GUIMPE

Tableau couvrant le folio 34b avec la scène »Purification«. Manuscrit enluminé.

Laus Mariae de Konrad de Haimburk, vers 1364.

Prague, Bibliothèque du Musée national, cote XVI D 13.

Tableau n° 44. MANTEAU PASSE PAR-DESSUS LA TETE AVEC VOILE BLANC

Détail du personnage de Marie.

Crucifiement de Vyšší Brod, avant 1400.

Peinture en détrempe sur bois de chêne, H. 129,5 cm, L. 98 cm.

Prague, Galerie nationale.

Annexe XI.

Détail avec Marie, de la »Mise au tombeau« du Maître de Třeboň, vers 1380.

Tableau n° 45. DETAIL DE VETEMENT, AVEC MOTIFS DECORATIFS PLASTIQUES

Ste Barbe (entre 1357 et 1367).

Maître Théodoric.

Karlštejn, Chapelle de la Sainte Croix.

Le château de Karlštejn, fondé en 1348 par l'empereur Charles IV, comme trésor des joyaux de la couronne impériale, occupe une position particulière parmi les châteaux européens du moyen-âge, aussi bien par sa destination que par sa décoration intérieure concentrée en majeure partie dans les chapelles privées. La plus intéressante à ce point de vue est la décoration uniforme de la chapelle de la Sainte Croix, garnie de pierres fines, de stucs dorés et d'un cycle de 127 panneaux avec des personnages de saints, de saintes, d'anges et de prophètes, qui constituent, avec l'architecture, un tout indivisible.

Tableau n° 46. PORTRAIT D'ANNA DE SVIDNICE, TROISIEME EPOUSE DE L'EMPEREUR CHARLES IV, VERS 1380

Grès avec les restes d'une vielle polychromie.

Partie d'un cycle de portraits avec 21 bustes, installé dans le triforium de la cathédrale de St Guy de Prague. L'initiateur du cycle fut probablement Charles IV.

Les bustes viennent de l'atelier de St Guy, qui travaillait sous l'influence de Pierre Arler, second architecte et sculpteur de cette église.

Tableau n° 47. PORTRAIT DE JEANNE DE BAVIERE, PREMIERE EPOUSE DE VENCESLAS IV, MORTE EN 1386

Grès. Voir les détails au n° 46.

Installé sur le côté ouest de la partie du triforium de St Guy qui se trouve au-dessus de la chapelle St Jean Népomucène, au sud de la clôture polygonale du choeur de la cathédrale St Guy de Prague.

Tableau n° 48. PORTRAIT D'ELISABETH DE PREMYSL, EPOUSE DE JEAN DE LUXEMBOURG, MORTE EN 1330

Grès. Voir tableau 46.

Le portrait a été exécuté entre 1375 et 1378. C'est donc un portrait posthume, tandis que les autres bustes sont exécutés d'après des modèles vivants.

Installé dans la galerie du triforium de la cathédrale St Guy à Prague.

Tableau n° 49. DETAIL DU VETEMENT D'UN SAINT EVEQUE AVEC, COMME MOTIF PEINT, UN LOTUS STYLISE

Maître Théodoric. Voir tableau n° 45.

Panneau de la chapelle de la Sainte Croix à Karlštejn.

254

Tableau n° 50. PORTRAIT DE BLANCHE DE VALOIS, PREMIERE EPOUSE
DE L'EMPEREUR CHARLES IV

Grès. Voir tableau 46.

Installé sur le côté sud du triforium, au-dessus de la chapelle de Saint Jean-Baptiste, au nord de la clôture
polygonale du choeur de la cathédrale St Guy à Prague.

Tableau n° 51. DETAIL DE L'ETOFFE DU VETEMENT DE STE OTILIE AVEC,
POUR MOTIF DECORATIF, DES CARRES PLASTIQUES DISPOSES
DE BIAIS ET UNE AGRAFE

Peinture en détrempe sur bois.

Maître Théodoric. Voir tableau 45.

Panneau central dans la chapelle de la Sainte Croix à Karlštejn.

Tableau n° 52. MANTEAU AVEC CAPUCHON ET VOILE

Détail du tableau »La Madone de St Guy«, vers 1400.

Peinture en détrempe sur bois, $51 \times 39,5$.

Le tableau était probablement destiné à l'église St Guy de Prague. Vers 1850, il fut complété par des améthystes dans l'auréole (sur notre fragment, le tableau est débarrassé de ces améthystes à la suite d'une restauration moderne).

Prague, Galerie nationale.

Tableau n° 53. MANTEAU A CAPE AVEC VOILE

Détail du tableau »La Madone de Zlatá Koruna«, exécuté vers 1410.

Peinture en détrempe sur bois, $68,5 \times 50$.

Le tableau était probablement destiné au monastère des cisterciens, à Zlatá Koruna. Ce monastère fut fondé
en 1263 par Přemysl Otakar II, comme symbole de la puissance royale contre la puissance des seigneurs
féodaux representée, dans le sud de la Bohême, par les Rožemberk.

Au XIV⁰ siècle, lorsque le panneau a été commandé, le monastère représentait un puissant bastion du pouvoir
clérical. Le tableau est aujourd'hui déposé à Prague dans la Galerie nationale.

Tableau n° 54. COIFFURE MODERNE, VOILE ET GUIMPE DE SAINTE
HELENE ET DE SA COMPAGNE

Retable de Rajhrad. Détail du tableau »La découverte et l'examen de la Sainte Croix« avant 1420.

Peinture en détrempe sur bois d'épicéa, 97×60. Probablement de la main d'un maître morave.

Partie de six tableaux du cycle de la Passion et de la légende de la Sainte Croix du Maître du retable de Rajhrad.
Au 19⁰ siècle, les six tableaux ont été déposés au couvent des Bénédictains à Rajhrad, en Moravie, d'où est
tiré le nom du maître, lequel était d'origine morave.

Brno, Musée morave.

Tableau n° 55. DETAIL DE L'ETOFFE AVEC MOTIFS DECORATIFS
DU VETEMENT DE LA MADONE A L'ENFANT JESUS

Voir tableau n° 36.

Partie centrale du triptyque avec la Madone, St Venceslas et St Palmacius.

Ecole italienne, 1357—1367.

Peinture en détrempe sur bois.

Le tableau fut commandé en Italie par Charles IV à l'occasion de son couronnement; il l'a installé au-dessus du
sanctuaire de la chapelle de la Sainte Croix à Karlštejn.

Annexe XII.

BROCARTS DE SOIE, BRODERIES ET ETOFFES PEINTES
Détail.
La »Madone de Kladsko«, vers 1350.
Peinture en détrempe sur bois de peuplier, 186×95.
Centre d'un retable disparu offert par le premier archevêque de Prague, Arnošt de Pardubice (représenté sur le panneau en tant que donateur), au monastère des augustins de Kladsko. D'où le titre du tableau.
Berlin, Deutsches Museum.

Tableau n° 56. DETAIL DE LA MANCHE DE BROCART AVEC MANCHETTES DECORATIVES DE LA MADONE DE STRAHOV
Maître tchèque vers 1350.
Peinture en détrempe sur bois, 94×84.
Ancienne propriété du monastère des prémontrés de Strahov à Prague.
Prague, Galerie nationale.

Tableau n° 57. DETAIL DE LA MANCHE DE BROCART
de la Madone dans le tableau du Maître de Vyšší Brod »La Nativité«. Voir tableau n° 25 et annexe.

Tableau n° 58. DETAIL D'UNE MANCHE ET D'UNE MANCHETTE DECORATIVE DE LA MADONE DE MOST
Voir annexe XIII.

Annexe XIII.

La Madone de Most, avant 1350.
Peinture en détrempe sur bois de peuplier, 53×40.
De 1578 à nos jours, dans l'église du monastère des Capucins à Most, en Bohême occidentale.

Tableau n° 59. COUPE ET PARURE (BOUTONS ET CEINTURE) D'UN VETEMENT GOTHIQUE DU MILIEU DU XIVE SIECLE
Détail, avec les figures d'un ange et des trois Maries, de la Résurrection, vers 1350.
Maître de Vyšší Brod.
Voir tableau n° 22 et annexe III.

Tableau n° 60. DETAIL DU VETEMENT ET DE LA MANCHE SIMPLE D'UN APOTRE,
dans la scène du Maître de Vyšší Brod »La Descente du Saint Esprit«. Voir annexe II.

Tableau n° 61. ROBE GOTHIQUE TRADITIONNELLE
Détail de la Madone avec St Barthélémy et Ste Marguerite, vers 1400.
Peinture en détrempe sur bois, 110×125.
Peint sans doute à l'origine pour l'église de Krumlov en Bohême méridionale, plus tard transféré dans le château néogothique de Hluboká, en Bohême du Sud.

Tableau n° 62. DETAIL D'UNE MANCHE SIMPLE DU TABLEAU DE S^{TE} HEDVIKA, DE MAITRE THEODORIC
Voir tableau 45.
Panneau dans la chapelle de la Sainte Croix de Karlštejn.

Tableau n° 63. DETAIL DU VETEMENT DE Ste CATHERINE, AVEC UNE ETOFFE AUX MOTIFS EN PARTIE EN RELIEF

Maître Théodoric. Voir annexe XIV.

Annexe XIV.

Tableau de Ste Catherine.
Peinture en détrempe sur bois, 114,5×87. Maître Théodoric. Voir tableau n° 45.
Panneau de la chapelle de la Sainte Croix à Karlštejn.

Tableau n° 64. DETAIL DU VETEMENT DE S^t GUY

Maître Théodoric.
Peinture en détrempe sur bois, 114×93.
Prague, Galerie nationale.

Tableau n° 65. DETAIL D'UN MOTIF PLASTIQUE PEINT DU VETEMENT DE Ste AGNES

Maître Théodoric. Pour plus de détails voir n° 45.
Premier panneau de gauche dans la chapelle de la Sainte Croix à Karlštejn.

Tableau n° 66—67. DETAIL DU VETEMENT DE SAINT STEPHANE, AVEC OURLET PEINT EN RELIEF

Maître Théodoric. Voir tableau n° 45.
Panneau de la chapelle de la Sainte Croix à Karlštejn.

Tableau n° 68. DETAIL DU COL DU SAINT PAPE CLEMENT

Maître Théodoric. Voir tableau n° 45.
Premier panneau de gauche dans la chapelle de la Sainte Croix à Karlštejn.

Tableau n° 69. MOTIF PLASTIQUE PEINT DU VETEMENT DE Ste MARGUERITE

Maître Théodoric. Voir tableau n° 45.
Panneau de la chapelle de la Sainte Croix à Karlštejn.

Tableau n° 70. DETAIL DE L'ORNEMENT DU COL DANS LE TABLEAU DE St AUGUSTIN

Maître Théodoric. Voir tableau n° 45.
Panneau de la chapelle de la Sainte Croix à Karlštejn.

Tableau n° 71. DETAIL DU VETEMENT ET DE L'ORNEMENTATION PLASTIQUE DU TABLEAU D'UN SAINT EVEQUE

Maître Théodoric. Voir tableau n° 45.
Panneau central dans la chapelle de la Sainte Croix à Karlštejn.

Tableau n° 72. DETAIL DE L'ETOFFE, DES JOYAUX ET DES PARURES DU VETEMENT, DANS LE TABLEAU D'UN SAINT EVEQUE

Maître Théodoric. Voir tableau n° 45.
Panneau de la chapelle de la Sainte Croix à Karlštejn.

Tableau n° 73. DETAIL DES JOYAUX DU VETEMENT DE S^T PALMACIUS, DANS LA PARTIE CENTRALE DU TRIPTYQUE:

La Madone avec St Venceslas et St Palmacius.

Ecole italienne, 1357—1367.

Tomasso da Modena.

Peinture en détrempe sur bois. Voir tableau n°s 36 et 55.

Tableau n° 74. LA BIBLE DE VENCESLAS IV

Les enluminures représentent le roi Venceslas avec une baigneuse.

Bible en six parties, inachevée, enluminée, en langue allemande, appartenant au groupe dit des manuscrits de Venceslas. La bible a été procurée à Venceslas IV par le maître-monnayeur Rotlev entre 1390 et 1400. La bible est richement ornementée de volutes complexes, peuplées d'animaux fantastiques, d'interprétations allégoriques et symboliques de diverses idées. M. Rotlev est sans doute issu d'une vieille famille bourgeoise de Prague, laquelle tire son nom de la maison »U černého lva« (ad ruffum leonem-maison du lion noir). La famille des Rotlev s'est inscrite dans l'histoire de Prague par le fait que leur maison du coin de la rue Železná, à Prague, devint la propriété du roi Venceslas IV, qui la céda en 1383 à l'Université de Prague.

Les relations intimes entre Rotlev et le roi sont attestées non seulement par une série de blasons qui ornent l'édifice du Carolinum à Prague, mais aussi par l'enluminure de notre bible qui, parmi les manuscrits enluminés du moyen-âge, est assez particulière, celui qui l'avait commandée s'étant efforcé d'aller au devant des prédilections et du goût de son roi. La bible est richement ornée de symboles — un martin-pêcheur et un rameau, un seau et des baigneuses.

Aujourd'hui le livre est conservé à Vienne, à la Bibliothèque d'Etat, cote Codex 2759—2764.

Tableaux n°s 75—81. LES ROBES LES PLUS SIMPLES DES BAIGNEUSES DE LA FIN DU XIVE SIECLE

Décor de volutes, dans le deuxième tome de la bible de Venceslas IV.

Tableau n° 82. CHEMISE DE NUIT DE LA FIN DU XIVE SIECLE

Detail de la naissance de Samson au folio 34 du deuxième volume de la bible de Venceslas IV.

Tableau n° 83. CHEMISE DE NUIT DE LA FIN DU XIVE SIECLE

Détail de la naissance de Samson, dans le deuxième volume de la bible de Venceslas IV, folio 17.

Tableau n° 84. ROBES DE BAIGNEUSES ETROITES, SANS EPAULETTES

Détail de l'initiale »D« avec une miniature montrant le roi parmi les baigneuses, folio 174 du premier volume de la bible de Venceslas IV.

Tableau n° 85. ROBES ETROITES DE BAIGNEUSES, AVEC EPAULETTES ET AVEC FILET SUR LA TETE

Détail d'une miniature montrant le roi avec des baigneuses, dans la bible de Venceslas IV.

Tableau n° 86. ROBES DE BAIGNEUSES ORNEES D'ECHARPES

Détail de bordure avec baigneuses, au folio 57 du troisième volume de la bible de Venceslas IV.

Tableau n° 87. Détail de bordure avec baigneuses, au folio 33 du deuxième volume de la bible de Venceslas IV.

Tableau n° 88. ROBES DE DAMES AGEES DE LA FIN DU XIVE SIECLE

Détail de la miniature »Samson s'en va avec ses parents à Tamnat«, au folio 18 du deuxième volume de la bible de Venceslas IV.

Tableau n° 89. ROBES ETROITES DE SOCIETE AVEC GRAND DECOLLETE, DE LA FIN DU XIVE SIECLE

Détail de la miniature »Dalila et Samson«, au folio 20 du deuxième volume de la bible de Venceslas IV.

Tableau n° 90. ROBE DE VILLE ETROITE DES BAIGNEUSES DE PRAGUE AVEC GRAND DECOLLETE

Baigneuses dans les volutes du deuxième volume de la bible de Venceslas IV.

Tableau n° 91. MANTEAUX ET ROBES DE SOCIETE AVEC LES ACCESSOIRES LES PLUS MODERNES (SOULIERS POINTUS)

L'initiale »H« du manuscrit de Guillaume d'Orange, 1387.

Tableau n° 92. ROBES DE BAIGNEUSES PRAGOISES ORNEES D'ECHARPES FLOTTANTES A LA TAILLE ET SUR LA TETE

Baigneuses dans les volutes du deuxième volume de la bible de Venceslas IV.

Tableau n° 93. ROBE DE CEREMONIE ELEGANTE DE LA FIN DU XIVE SIECLE AVEC ECHARPES FLOTTANTES ET LARGES MANCHES

Détail de Bulla Aurea Caroli IV regis.
Le manuscrit latin enluminé, datant de 1390—1400, appartenait à la bibliothèque de Venceslas IV.
Détail d'une miniature avec le roi, la reine et trois vierges, au folio 33.
Vienne, Bibliothèque d'Etat, cote Codex 338.

Tableau n° 94. MOTIFS DECORATIFS DES ROBES DE BAIGNEUSES AVEC TOUS LES DETAILS

Détail de l'initiale »U« avec baigneuse au folio 108 du deuxième volume de la bible de Venceslas IV.

Tableau n° 95. Voir tableau n° 94.

L'initiale »U« avec baigneuse au folio 130 du premier volume de la bible de Venceslas IV.

Tableau n° 96. ROBES DE BAIGNEUSES AVEC CEINTURE SUR LES HANCHES, BONNET ET CHEVEUX DEFAITS

L'initiale »U« avec baigneuses, au folio 112 du troisième volume de la bible de Venceslas IV.

Tableaux n°s 97 et 98. REVUE DES ROBES DE SOCIETE LES PLUS DIVERSES DE LA FIN DU XIVE SIECLE

Détail de la miniature »Marie, la soeur d'Aron, avec des femmes«, au folio 69 du deuxième livre de Moïse, de la bible de Venceslas IV.

Tableau n° 99. ROBES ETROITES A BOUTONS ET VOILES D'APRES LA DERNIERE MODE DU XIVE SIECLE

Guillaume d'Orange.
Détail d'une miniature.
Vienne, Bibliothèque d'Etat (Code AN).

Tableau n° 100. MODELE DE BROCART GOTHIQUE

Détail de la couverture de la Mort de la Vierge Marie.
Retable de Roudnice, vers 1410.
Peinture en détrempe sur bois, $147 \times 118,5$.
Le retable fut vraisemblablement peint pour l'église de la Vierge Marie à Roudnice.
Prague, Galerie nationale.

Tableau n° 113. ROBE MAGNIFIQUE ORNEE DE PERLES ET DE FOURRURE DE LA FIN DU XIVᴱ SIECLE

Détail d'une miniature avec l'ange annonçant à Manuel et à sa femme la naissance de Samson, au folio 17 du deuxième volume de la Bible de Venceslas IV.

Tableau n° 114. ROBE AVEC SURCOT ET GUIMPE

Détail de l'enluminure de la Bible de Venceslas IV.

Tableaux n°ˢ 115—116. MANTEAU ROYAL DE CEREMONIE AVEC CAPE ET »KOGEL« BOHEMIEN

Détail de l'initiale »D« du manuscrit de Guillaume d'Orange (1387).

Tableau n° 117. Détail avec la reine Sophie, femme de Venceslas IV, assise sur le trône, deuxième volume de la Bible de Venceslas IV.

Tableau n° 118. Détail avec baigneuse assise dans les volutes, au folio 130 de la Bible de Venceslas IV.

Tableau n° 119. VETEMENT DE TRAVAIL DU MILIEU DU XIVᴱ SIECLE

Detail avec une sage femme. Illustration dessinée. Bible de Velislav, avant le milieu du XIVᵉ siècle.

Tableau n° 120. ECHANTILLON SIMPLE DE TEXTILE

Détail du vêtement de Jésus dans le tableau de la Madone de Březnice de la fin du XVᵉ siècle.
Peinture en détrempe sur bois, 41 × 29,5.
Prague, Galerie nationale.

Tableau n° 121. VETEMENTS DE TRAVAIL DE LA FIN DU XIVᴱ SIECLE

Détail avec la mère, au folio 110 du premier volume de la Bible de Venceslas IV. Voir tableau 74.

Tableau n° 122. VETEMENT DE TRAVAIL DU MILIEU DU XVᴱ SIECLE

Détail du tableau de la Naissance, avec la sage femme, dont la robe a été repeinte.
Maître de Vyšší Brod, vers 1350.
Voir annexe II.

Tableau n° 123. Détail du drap de lit du manuscrit Liber viaticus, 1364.

Voir tableau n° 40.

Tableau n° 124. Détails avec drap de lit du recueil dit de Krumlov, qui contient des traités religieux.

Autres détails au folio 9.
Voir tableau n° 4.

Tableau n° 125. DETAIL D'UN DRAP ET D'UNE COUVERTURE DE LIT.

Folio 9 de l'Almanach de Krumlov. Traités sur la religion, voir n° 4 et 124.

Tableau n° 126. DETAIL DU DRAP DE LIT DE LA MORT DE LA VIERGE MARIE DE BRNO

Peinture en détrempe sur bois d'aune, 33,8 × 24.
Elle fut vraisemblablement exécutée dans un atelier de Moravie vers 1390.
Brno, Musée morave.

Tableau n° 127 et annexe XV. »Bénie soit Agnès la tutélaire«.

Ce tableau fait partie du retable de Nicolas Puchner, grand-maître de l'ordre des Crosiers à l'étoile rouge, qui le commanda pour l'autel principal de l'église jadis gothique de Saint François de la Vieille Ville de Prague.
Prague, Galerie nationale.

Annexe XVI.

MANTEAUX AVEC COLS

Détail avec Ste Dorothée et Ste Apolena.

Cadre de la Madone de St Thomas, vers 1420.

Peinture en détrempe sur bois de tilleul.

Le tableau provient de l'église de St Thomas de Brno.

Brno, Musée Morave.

Tableau n° 137. MANTEAU AVEC COL

La Visitation dite de Ringhoffer, après 1430.

Peinture en détrempe sur bois, 100×70.

Fragment de l'arche de l'autel, reliant vraisemblablement le cycle de Marie à celui de la Passion, attribué au Maître du Chemin de Croix de Vyšší Brod.

Prague, Galerie nationale.

Annexe XVII.

MANTEAU AVEC COL

Assomption de Lanna, vers 1450.

Peinture en détrempe sur bois de pin, 41,5×31,5, avec le cadre peint original.

Le tableau figurait dans la collection du collectionneur praguois V. Lanna, qui l'avait acheté en 1883.

Prague, Galerie nationale.

Tableau n° 138.

Salomé avec la tête de St Jean.

Arche de Zátoň, après 1430.

Peinture en détrempe sur bois d'épicéa, largeur 42.

Volet droit d'un triptyque, avec l'encadrement original.

Le retable provient de l'église St Jean-Baptiste de Zátoň, dans le sud de la Bohême.

Prague, Galerie nationale.

Annexe XVIII.

Détail de Salomé du retable de Zátoň. Voir tableau n° 138.

Tableau n° 139. MODELE DE TEXTILE REPRODUISANT LE VELOURS

Détail de robe de l'Assomption de Deštná, avec grenades pour motif (le plus ancien échantillon de ce modèle conservé chez nous).

Peinture en détrempe sur bois de pin, 114×111.

Prague, Galerie nationale.

Tableau n° 140. LE LAÇAGE

Peinture sur le cadre de bois de la Madone de Vyšší Brod (type de St Guy), vers 1460.

Détail avec Ste Marguerite.

Le tableau provient peut-être de l'église de la Vierge Marie de Vyšší Brod. Il se trouve à présent dans l'ancienne galerie du monastère.

Annexe XIX.

MANCHETTES POST-GOTHIQUES ET DECOLLETE RENAISSANCE

Détail de la Décapitation de Ste Barbe, après 1540. Partie centrale d'un triptyque provenant vraisemblablement de l'église du monastère de l'Assomption à Osek, attribué au maître I. W. et à son aide.

Prague, Galerie nationale.

Tableau n° 141. TENUE DE TRAVAIL DES VENDEUSES DU MARCHE
DE LA VILLE

Détail de la feuille »La vie dans les montagnes«, après 1490, du Graduel de Kutná Hora (manuscrit enluminé).
Dans le graduel est reflétée la vie des mineurs, avec des scènes de la vie quotidienne, tout à fait réalistes.
Vienne, Bibliothèque d'Etat.

Tableau n° 142. VETEMENT DE TRAVAIL DE VILLE AVEC TABLIER

Détail de la feuille »La vie dans les montagnes«, après 1490.
Graduel de Kutná Hora. Voir n° 141.

Tableau n° 143. COIFFURE RENAISSANCE

Kutná Hora, église de Ste Barbe.
Détail d'une scène sur le mur oriental, en haut, avec la Sibylle de Tiburtin, montrant à l'empereur Augustin
la Madone et lui annonçant l'arrivée du Sauveur.
Peinture murale de la chapelle Smíšek, 1490.
Kutná Hora, autrefois village de mineurs, est devenue, sous le règne de Venceslas II (1278—1305), une sorte
de »Californie tchèque«. Jusqu'à la Renaissance, cette ville minière, riche en gisements d'argent, a rapidement
grandi. Pour répondre au désir de la ville orgueilleuse, on eut l'idée de construire l'église de la patronne des
mineurs, Ste Barbe. Parmi les bourgeois de Kutná Hora, monsieur Smíšek de Vrchoviště occupe une place importante. Son nom a été donné à l'une des chapelles de la cathédrale de Ste Barbe.

Tableau n° 144. MODELE D'ECHANTILLON DE TEXTILE DE LA RENAISSANCE,
AVEC LA GRENADE POUR MOTIF DECORATIF

Détail du »Couronnement de la Vierge Marie« du retable d'Osek, vers 1520.
Peinture sur bois de tilleul, $150,5 \times 100,5$.
Partie centrale du triptyque démonté.
Prague, Galerie nationale.

Tableau n° 145. MODELE DE TEXTILE DE LA RENAISSANCE AVEC
LA GRENADE COMME MOTIF DECORATIF

Détail de l'Annonciation, peinture de la fin du X Ve siècle.
Rakovník, Musée municipal.

Tableau n° 146. BERET RENAISSANCE

Détail de peinture murale de la scène »Le Crucifiement«, vers 1490.
Kutná Hora, église Ste Barbe, chapelle Smíšek. Voir tableau n° 143.

Tableau n° 147. CHASUBLE DE LA RENAISSANCE EN SAMIT (ORIGINAL),
PROVENANT DE BUDYN SUR L'OHRE

Prague, Musée national.

Tableau n° 148. ENCOLURE, COIFFURE ET PORT DU BERET

Marie-Madeleine de Malý Bor, près de Horažďovice, vers 1520.
Détail, bois plastique.
České Budějovice, Musée municipal.

Tableau n° 149. COIFFURE SOUS LA RENAISSANCE

Détail de »La Sibylle de Tiburtin«.
Kutná Hora, église de Ste Barbe, chapelle Smíšek.
Voir tableaux n°s 143 et 146.

Tableau n° 150. V E T E M E N T D E C E R E M O N I E D E L A R E N A I S S A N C E

Détail de la scène »Passage de la reine de Saba à travers les eaux«, vers 1490. Voir n° 153.
Kutná Hora, église Ste Barbe, chapelle Smíšek.

Tableau n° 151. C O I F F U R E R E N A I S S A N C E

Détail de »La reine de Saba«, vers 1490.

Tableau n° 152. B E R E T D E L A R E N A I S S A N C E E T E N C O L U R E

Détail de la scène »La justice de Trajan«, vers 1490.
Voir tableaux n°s 143, 146, 149, 150, 153.
Kutná Hora, église Ste Barbe, chapelle Smíšek.

Tableau n° 153. V E T E M E N T S D E V I L L E S O U S L A R E N A I S S A N C E

Détail de la peinture murale de la scène »Passage de la Reine de Saba à travers les eaux«, vers 1490.
Voir tableaux n°s 143, 146, 149.
Kutná Hora, église Ste Barbe, chapelle Smíšek.

PHOTOGRAPHS BY

Z. Feyfar
Nos. 3, 4, 38—41, 43, 123—125

J. Ehm
Nos. 5, 20—26, 29, 30, 32—34, 56, 57, 60, 64, 120, 122, 127, 137—139, 141,
142, 144

STÁTNÍ FOTOMĚŘICKÝ ÚSTAV
Nos. 1, 19, 31, 35, 42, 44, 52, 53, 54, 61, 74, 75—99, 101—106, 109—118, 121,
128, 129, 131, 133, 140, 147

V. Hnízdo
Nos. 2, 27, 28, 100

F. Illek and A. Paul
Nos. 6—18, 36, 37, 45—51, 55, 62, 63, 65—73, 107, 108, 119, 130,
132, 134, 135, 143, 145, 146, 149—153

Orbis 2
Nos. 58, 59, 126, 136, 148